Mohammed VI's Strategies for Moroccan Economic Development

This book analyzes the economic development choices initiated by Morocco's King Mohammed VI since he ascended the throne in 1999 and situates those choices in the political economy development literature.

Examining the policies enacted by the King, the authors argue that over the past 20 years Mohammed VI has achieved some outstanding successes in modernizing the foundational economic sectors of Morocco, but the benefits of this development have not reached all Moroccans. With its focus on economic development, this book explores the way in which Mohammed VI's development strategies have, in part, resembled the neoliberal model advocated by Western powers and institutions, as well as how the King also adopted some of the European practices of state intervention found in the "varieties of capitalism" models across Europe. Additionally, *Mohammed VI's Strategies for Moroccan Economic Development* investigates the way in which the King has sought to utilize "leapfrog" technologies so that Morocco has become a leader in certain productive sectors and is not just catching up to rival producers. The book also examines the extent to which Moroccan citizens have benefited from the economic transformations, arguing that not all Moroccans have benefited; many Moroccan citizens in 2019 echo the same economic concerns that were voiced in 1999 when King Mohammed VI first assumed the throne.

With its focus on economic development, this book will be of interest to scholars and students of not only Middle East and North African Studies but also Economics, International Development, and Politics.

Eve Sandberg is Professor of Politics at Oberlin College, Oberlin, Ohio, USA.

Seth Binder is Advocacy Officer at the Project on Middle East Democracy (POMED), Washington DC, USA.

Routledge African Studies

For a full list of available titles please visit: https://www.routledge.com/African-Studies/book-series/AFRSTUD

Mohammed VI's Strategies for Moroccan Economic Development

Eve Sandberg and Seth Binder

LONDON AND NEW YORK

First published 2020 by Routledge

2 Park Square, Milton Park, Abingdon, Oxon, OX14 4RN
605 Third Avenue, New York, NY 10017

Routledge is an imprint of the Taylor & Francis Group, an informa business

First issued in paperback 2020

British Library Cataloguing-in-Publication Data
A catalogue record for this book is available from the British Library

Library of Congress Cataloging-in-Publication Data
Names: Sandberg, Eve, author. | Binder, Seth, author.
Title: Mohammed VI's strategies for Moroccan economic development / Eve Sandberg and Seth Binder.
Description: New York : Routledge, 2019. | Series: Routledge African studies ; 32 | Includes bibliographical references and index.
Identifiers: LCCN 2019016508 (print) | LCCN 2019017694 (ebook) | ISBN 9781351065986 (Ebook) | ISBN 9781351065979 (Adobe Reader) | ISBN 9781351065962 (Epub) | ISBN 9781351065955 (Mobipocket) | ISBN 9781138479333 (hardback)
Subjects: LCSH: Economic development—Morocco. | Morocco—Politics and government—1999– | Morocco—Economic policy. | Morocco—Economic conditions.
Classification: LCC HC810 (ebook) | LCC HC810 .S26 2019 (print) | DDC 338.96409049—dc23
LC record available at https://lccn.loc.gov/2019016508

ISBN: 978-1-138-47933-3 (hbk)
ISBN: 978-0-367-78473-7 (pbk)

Typeset in Times New Roman
by codeMantra

Eve Sandberg dedicates this book to Sandra Zagarell who continues to offer support and encouragement for all of Eve's endeavors and Eve only hopes that she returns this support in kind. Eve also thanks Kasha, Nina, and Kingston for providing such a warm environment for reflection and writing.

Seth Binder dedicates this book to Allison Avolio whose love, strength, and compassion continue to be an inspiration. He would also like to thank all those who have supported him along the way.

Contents

Acknowledgments

Getting a manuscript ready for publication often requires support from many sources. The authors would like to thank the staff at the Oberlin College library for assistance in securing often difficult-to-acquire source materials. They particularly thank librarians Allison Gallaher, Jessica Grim, Michael McFarlin, and Diane Lee. Additionally, they thank Sandy Austen of the Center for Information and Technology of Oberlin College for her technical assistance while they were writing the manuscript. Finally, Eve Sandberg would like to thank the Research Status Award Committee of Oberlin College and those who administer the Powers Travel Grant, for funding her general project studies of Morocco's evolving political economy.

1 Mohammed VI ascends to the throne in 1999 facing critical choices for Moroccan development

At the end of the 1990s, the winds of democracy were blowing globally. Additionally, many around the world were demanding economic advancement – demanding not to be left out of the new benefits of globalization and at the same time to be shielded from its dangers. In Morocco, then governed by King Hassan II, many saw economic improvement and democratic governance as linked endeavors. Morocco was a monarchy, however, and Hassan was not about to abdicate nor embrace true democratic reforms. Further, after decades of neglect of the country's economy, Hassan had abandoned his import substitution policies and instead embraced various neoliberal approaches to development in exchange for much-needed loans from the officials at the Bretton Woods Institutions (BWIs) – the International Monetary Fund (IMF) and the World Bank. As he modified his economic policies, Hassan II also allowed Morocco's opposition political parties to form a parliamentary bloc, and then he chose a socialist party leader as Prime Minister. But the King retained control of the budget, the police, and the military, as well as the choice of Cabinet Ministers that comprised Morocco's Executive branch of government.

While many Moroccans were proud of their royalty and its traditions as well as proud of the "Moroccan exceptionalism" that distinguished their country from their Middle East and North African (MENA) neighbors, in the later part of the 1990s, many Moroccans also aspired to improve their lives economically and longed for freedom of speech and freedom in public spaces. But Moroccans had little hope of far-reaching change through existing parliamentary politics, so they could only hope for their King to permit a greater role for the country's political parties and to give more attention to economic initiatives that might benefit those Moroccans who lacked personal access to the royal family, to those around them, and/or to the King's advisors. (Those close to the King are known as the "Makhzen.") Therefore, when King Hassan II died in July 1999, after ruling Morocco for 38 years, many Moroccans looked to his son Mohammed VI, who inherited the throne, to introduce the changes to Morocco's political economy that would lead to improved economic and political conditions in Morocco.

Mohammed VI became Morocco's Head of State about one month before his 36th birthday. He had received both modern academic and practical workforce experience that few other monarchs had enjoyed.[1] Additionally, like other monarchs of the modern age, Mohammed VI was aware of the fate of the Shah of Iran who, 20 years earlier, having neglected the welfare of his subjects was driven from his throne. On becoming Morocco's new King, Mohammed VI signaled that he intended to bring real political and economic change to Morocco, but he simultaneously adopted practices that let it be known that he also intended to play a major role in the next phase of Morocco's development and its governance structures.

The new monarch continued some of his father's recent efforts at neoliberal reform, but he immediately began planning for an accelerated phase in Morocco's political democratization and economic growth. However, the King was facing enormous challenges, especially in bringing about economic development.

This study therefore asks, after 20 years of rule (1999–2019), how have His Majesty Mohammed VI's economic plans (enacted and then modified over time) affected the fortunes of Moroccan citizens and how successful are the economic sectors that the King targeted for development? This is the empirical question that we ask and answer in this work. Additionally, we contextualize our findings on the Moroccan case in the important theoretical debates of economic development. For these debates, Morocco provides an insightful case study and allows us to make a contribution to the development literatures.

Empirically, we argue that Mohammed VI has achieved some outstanding successes in modernizing certain sectors of Morocco's economy and in professionalizing some areas in which Moroccans work. For example, both Morocco's finance and telecommunications sectors have developed in ways that improved the lives of many Moroccans, and these upgraded areas provide an important foundation on which Morocco can receive and manage additional, often foreign, investment that is needed to spur development across the economy. But it is difficult to modernize a country in only 20 years – to move a country from a largely pre-capitalist formation to an industrial and financial hub. Unsurprisingly, then, we argue that for the majority of Moroccans, little has changed during this King's reign even though much has been accomplished. Our findings track with the UN Human Development Index that in 1999 ranked Morocco 126 on its development index, and then in 2018, 19 years into King Mohammed VI's reign, Morocco was ranked 123 of 189 countries on the UN Human Development Index.[2]

Moreover, although important pockets of development have occurred in various parts of the country, in those areas where Morocco's development efforts over the past 20 years have had little impact, citizens are bitter. Many recognize that they are being left behind and that they have little prospect of seeing in their lifetimes the changes to which they aspire.

Twenty years after Mohammed VI ascended to the throne, and despite many positive changes across parts of the country, many Moroccan citizens in 2019 echo many of the concerns that were voiced in 1999 when King Mohammed VI first assumed his duties. To be sure, Morocco's middle class has expanded in the past two decades. For example, in 2009, Morocco's High Commissioner for Planning claimed that 53% of Moroccans had achieved middle-class status, whereas another 13% were upper class. The Moroccan middle class was said to earn about $633 monthly which put it over the median of earners in Morocco.[3] However, it is obvious that for a population living in a global economy, this salary does not provide for the kind of middle-class comfort experienced in other parts of the world. Further, we find that where previously many Moroccans had little contact with how others outside their country lived, now with Morocco's highly successful telecommunications and internet sectors, many Moroccans are well aware of their lives within the context of the global economy. Thus, as we shall demonstrate across Morocco's economic landscape, there has been good success in just 20 years, but that good success does not offer much comfort to most Moroccan citizens, even to many of those who are said to have succeeded.

We also find that the King's policies have, to some degree, sought to create a demand structure *within* Morocco. This provides a necessary balance against the risk of Morocco's producing almost solely for export and being at the mercy of external events.[4] And another hedge against the vagaries of the international market can be seen in recent years when King Mohammed VI aggressively pursued a policy of diversifying the products Morocco exported as well as Morocco's export destinations. Yet, there remains an imbalance whereby Morocco relies on external economic transactions, and this threatens Morocco's economic security and jeopardizes the national well-being. We note that after 20 years, during times of international economic crisis, Morocco possesses few levers by which to buffer its economy and its people. Creating more domestic linkages for production, especially between urban and rural parts of the country, to boost sales internally should be an important component of Morocco's economic development strategy. Such a strategy will require some additional deviation from the laissez-faire model; few domestic or foreign investors are likely to invest in Morocco's remote rural areas. Yet, we argue, it is in the rural areas, or at least in their hubs, where a pragmatic leader must help to underwrite local investment for productive enterprises.

Regarding the development theories of the past 20 years, we argue that King Mohammed VI has fashioned a development policy for Morocco that, in part, resembled the neoliberal model advocated by Western powers and institutions, but importantly he also adopted some of the European practices of state intervention. While he has not particularly replicated any specific programs enacted in the "varieties of capitalism" models found across Europe, he clearly has embraced the right of the state to intervene in his country's economy. Further, we note that King Mohammed VI departed from neoliberal principles when the King believed that Moroccan domestic concerns required it. That King Mohammed VI is able to deviate from pressures to adopt pristine neoliberal policies stems, in part, from his role in international politics and his good standing among European and US leaders. There is no push in the West to see this King overthrown. Moreover, if he delays in implementing some of the BWI's policies, observers note that he already has implemented many of the BWI's prescribed policies. And this King maintains high-level contacts not only with key Western allies in the United States and Europe but also with regional allies, such as the Saudis. He also engages with Russia and China.

While Mohammed VI opened his economy and his country in a major way to neoliberal investment and production practices, the Moroccan state continues to play an active role as a competitor and/or as a partner in the (public) spheres of finance and development. This does not simply involve Keynesian fiscal regulation. Rather, the state has its own companies, makes its own investments, and oversees a private banking sector that is both regulated and encouraged to provide development financing for state-prioritized economic initiatives. Additionally, where privatization has occurred, often state firms have been sold to Royals (including the King it is alleged) or to those private citizens who are favored by the Royal family and their political allies. Finally, during his initial years of reign, the King adopted an almost exclusive sectoral approach for domestic development as well as a regional approach focused on the European Union (EU) for Morocco's economic outreach. In recent years, however, the King has come to see that regional development at home must be given attention as well. And the countries of origin for Morocco's exports and imports have begun to diversify.

In the political sphere, King Mohammed VI has been observed as playing the role of the "ultimate arbitrator and balancer between competing social and political forces" or as an "Executive Monarchy."[5] In the economic realm, Morocco's development goals and strategies now are largely animated by the King's ongoing activities, including traveling, treaty making, and transactional deal brokering. Morocco's King is not merely a ruler but also an active development entrepreneur on behalf of his country. There are few countries in which the head of state is as energetic and innovative as is Mohammed VI.

In Morocco, there are spaces for private sector entrepreneurs and also state-owned enterprises. There are also public–private partnerships (PPPs). Additionally, state policies target certain sectors to receive benefits and state support. Further, Mohammed VI adopted technologies that "leapfrogged" widespread existing technologies to gain greater returns for Moroccans. His famous development of Morocco's solar power is but one example of this (though with this initiative has come some unintended consequences).

We note, therefore, that Mohammed VI did not adopt a single grand strategy for economic development. As we will discuss in this chapter, import substitution industrialization, Soviet-style state planning, and the Washington

Consensus including the structural adjustment policies of the International Monetary Fund and the World Bank were largely discredited (except to their much-diminished numbers of true believers) when Mohammed VI assumed the throne. Rather the King focused on sectoral development and trade with Europe, and then broadened his trade outreach globally.

It is clear that the King believes that he has made economic choices for Morocco that ultimately will be successful. In his 2017 annual Throne Speech, despite widespread protests and unemployment, and despite the lack of evidence of substantial economic development for many Moroccans, the King argued that the country's economic policies were correct. He stated, "All in all, our development policy choices remain sound. The problem lies with mentalities that have not evolved as well as with the inability to implement projects and to innovate."[6] The King had become suspicious of those working in the public sector.

Additionally, the King also had become alert to the needs of those who were being left behind. In his Throne Speech in 2015, the King noted that "there is a category of the population still living in dire conditions and feeling marginalized, notwithstanding what has already been done."[7] It was also in 2015 that the King launched a new five-year development plan with an eye to historically disenfranchised regions of the country. Then, following the violent protests that broke out between 2016 and 2018, the King stepped back and suggested that it was Morocco's "political class" (in the words of commentator, Mohamed Daadaoui), not his policies that were obstructing development; in a stunning political action, the King fired five cabinet ministers for "serious dysfunctions" in implementing the country's development plans.[8]

But while the King is alert to those who have been left behind, and while he robustly pursues Morocco's economic development, he will not earn credit for his efforts if more is not done to improve the economic fortunes of the majority of Moroccans. The King cannot expect that Morocco can sustain two economies: one for the well-connected and the other for the have-nots. A nation's economic activities have ripple effects throughout any state and across its population. The wealth of those who have much must be captured in taxes and not be allowed to engage in capital flight. Morocco needs liquidity. The wealth of those who have much must be directed to uplift those who do not have. Only then will an analysis of the King's efforts yield a better report in the future.

The King's approach to Moroccan economic development can be characterized as a sort of imprecise adaptation of European capitalist economies in the 2000s, a capitalist economy that differed from the US model. As Bob Hancké argued, European "varieties of capitalism" "incorporates a strong sense of social justice with a larger role for the state and for regulation in the economy" as well as an "institutionalized balance of power between capital and labour" (which are mutually dependent), while guarding against inefficiencies in output.[9]

By 2010, about a decade into King Mohammed VI's reign, and in the wake of the Western economic crisis of 2008, a rising authoritarian China and an autocratic Vladimir Putin were propounding state-led development as the alternative to what they saw as failed neoliberal market-based development. As we shall demonstrate, Morocco's King maintained his partial neoliberal emphasis for Morocco's development strategies, but he also utilized state power and intervention when he believed it was necessary. In some ways, this reflects the approach that Joseph Stiglitz has argued helped China to develop so quickly. Importantly, however, Stiglitz notes that while the East Asian model supported development in targeted sectors, it simultaneously allowed an entrepreneurial space for thousands of citizens that propelled development and the diversification of production. Stiglitz also notes that the global financial crisis of 2008 cast doubt on the neoliberal paradigm for development in both late industrializing countries and countries with developed economies.[10] For Stiglitz, the task of economic policy-makers is to determine where and when the government should intervene, where to take risks to support new endeavors, and where and when to let the market work alone.[11] Additionally, he notes that economic planners must embrace the advancement of new technologies if their country's economy is to compete globally.[12]

Prior to the reign of Mohammed VI, in the late 1980s and during the 1990s, the World Bank experts witnessed many failed structural adjustment programs around the world causing a number of them to believe that market reform alone could not spur development. The World Bank experts began to argue that "good governance" was foundational for private sector liberalization to succeed. Trainings and the professionalization of a state's bureaucracy were necessary if market reform was to be achieved and national development attained.

But, as Mushtaq H. Khan has argued, those who contended that improving governance and bureaucratic skills – in order to avoid the inefficiencies of corruption and poor service delivery and to achieve market-enhancing governance – missed important understandings of the underlying causes of failed neoliberal programs.[13] Likewise, those who previously had argued that states should intervene to avoid market failures and better utilize scarce resources through government intervention, and sometimes import-substituting industrialization, also missed the appropriate role for state economic policy-makers and those in government who must implement policies.[14] Khan argued instead that, as was even noted by World Bank documents, East Asian states were successful due to some preexisting state capacities that went beyond market-enhancing governance and which should be the focus of international development experts.[15] However, Khan also noted that growth-enhancing governance practices differ country to country because the "precise nature of the governance capabilities required depends on the specific mechanisms through which the state attempts to accelerate technology, acquisition and investment."[16] As will be analyzed later in this volume, after ascending the throne, King Mohammed VI adopted strategies to professionalize key sectors of Morocco's economy, and to alter and enforce Moroccan laws to protect foreign and domestic investment.

With regard to the Moroccan case and its development theories, it is also interesting to note that many economic development experts have argued that the economically successful Asian states had emphasized producing for export markets in order to launch their development trajectories, and so other aspiring late developing countries should do the same. On a variation of this model, and lacking a population with much discretionary income, Mohammed VI sought foreign investment that would create production and jobs in Morocco for companies that planned to export at first almost exclusively in Europe, and only later in non-European expanding economies as well. In this study, we find that these approaches to development achieved some good success, but Morocco's development may well need deliberately planned production linkages between urban and rural areas, and between active and less active geographical areas within Morocco if the political stability necessary to attract and sustain foreign investment is to be achieved and if development is to bring benefits to all regions of Morocco.

When reviewing the King's development strategies, it appears that King Mohammed VI adopted policies from a range of perspectives. For example, the King adopted some policies in keeping with many development experts at the United Nations Conference on Trade and Development (UNCTAD) who believed that technology was key to economic progress. Rather than simply allowing free market operations to make technological decisions, late industrializing countries, where possible, should "leapfrog" in choosing technologies that their companies should adopt.

The King's decision to leapfrog to solar technology was a particularly good fit for Morocco because, as any observer can see, the sun – if harnessed – can serve as a major natural resource for the country which contains large tracts of the Saharan desert. But it probably did not hurt that the United Nations (UN) experts were promoting alternative and sustainable energy sources based on both economic and environmental grounds. And while the King invested heavily in solar, and in doing so attracted enthusiasm, he has also continued to invest in coal and oil production. The King also has attempted to leapfrog technology in the transport sector to position Morocco as a regional hub for natural gas transit, and also to import cheaper natural gas to fuel Morocco's phosphate industry in place of higher costing oil imports.[17]

Additionally, the King's role in bringing women into the public sphere, in response to decades of organizing by Moroccan women leaders, has been not just a human rights accomplishment and a hedge against radical Islamists but also a strategy that will aid development. In Morocco today, there are both economic and democratic opportunities for Moroccan women where previously there were few or none.[18] Not all Moroccan women have made gains. But many of the legal impediments to women's advancement have been mitigated, and where once a woman was prohibited from even attending a private meeting unescorted by a male, now women are to be found in all walks of life, working by themselves or in groups and energetically contributing to the development of their country.[19] And has been demonstrated elsewhere, when women's contributions to national development are increased, they play a catalyst role for improving the lives of men and boys, and in attaining national development goals. But gender equality should be "a core objective of development (goal) on its own."[20] Morocco's King Mohammed VI's strategies for development have clearly included women.

As we demonstrate in this volume, development strategies in Morocco also require citizen involvement because political and economic advancements are intertwined. For example, political stability is a key attraction to both foreign and domestic investors in both the manufacturing and industry sectors. The King's recognition of the need for some political reforms was clearly observed following the 2011 Arab Spring demonstrations across the country. King Mohammed VI made some adjustments to Morocco's political party system, yielding some personal powers to the parties. However, even with these reforms, the King reserved for himself, and likely for his heir, Crown Prince Moulay Hassan (born in 2003), the means by which to continue to dominate the affairs of the Kingdom, including its development strategies.

Because King Mohammed VI's national economic development strategies did not reach a majority of Moroccans to effectively alter their living conditions, the political components of Morocco's economic stability looms. Stability and worker productivity are necessary for economic growth. Lack of stability and workers' strikes, or worker slowdowns, threaten economic growth. Oppressed and desperate citizens will politically halt the wheels of economic activity if they do not experience economic improvement, or if they believe that they have no (economic or political) space to live their lives. With little to lose, they will turn against the existing system. The King has kept worker benefits low, employment during the past 20 years has not increased as fast as the King and his advisers had hoped, and economic desperation continues to cause protests and violence.

During the Arab Spring, 40 teachers protested in front of the Ministry of Education and tried to immolate themselves to demonstrate the lack of support they had received from the state since they had been sacked in 2008 as part of budget cuts. Five jobless college graduates set themselves on fire to protest unemployment during January 2012.[21]

Mohammed VI's political policies, to date, have suggested that he does not wish to govern through secret police and violence and through threatening the well-being of his citizenry as his father did. That he created in 2004 a Justice and Reconciliation Commission headed by a former political prisoner to investigate the violence and brutalities of his father's regime validates this intent. Unfortunately, other actions that he has taken in recent years contribute to a more mixed assessment.

Critics charge that Morocco's King is willing to protect human rights in general, but when his own interests are at stake, the King is not above the use of imprisonment as a political solution. For example, in June 2003, Ali Lmrabet, an editor of two Moroccan magazines, reported that tourist developers had arranged to purchase one of the King's palaces. Lmrabet quickly was sentenced to three years in jail for "insulting the king's person" and "undermining the monarchy."[22]

Yet, in the aftermath of the 2011–2012 Arab Spring, with huge protests in Morocco's major cities, as part of his announcement of a new political era, King Mohammed VI eliminated secret military courts so that citizens who now were accused of treason would have their cases heard in civilian, not military courts. While this still might preclude a fair trial for anyone reporting on the King's person, in terms of Moroccan practices it was seen as a reform. But unfortunately, there remained those certain national topics that were going to be responded to swiftly and ruthlessly.

For example, in 2013, it became clear that the new court dispensation would not extend to those who organized protests in the Western Sahara. Human Rights Watch (HRW) reported that a Moroccan military court had found 25 protesters guilty of violent resistance. These Sahrawis individuals were given sentences that ranged from several years in prison to life sentences (for nine of them). HRW observed that

> The court failed to probe the allegations made by defendants, most of whom had spent 26 months in pretrial detention, that police officers had tortured or coerced them into signing false statements. Yet, the court relied on these contested statements as the main, if not sole, evidence to convict them.[23]

It must be noted as well that 11 Moroccan service people died during the violent protests referenced above and that no country permits what it believes to be secessionist movements to operate without facing accusations of treason. But free and fair trials are essential.

In recent years, Morocco's King has called upon the military and police to maintain order and control when domestic protests have roiled the Kingdom. This has led to the increasing use of the police, detention, and legal accusations against the King's public critics. For example, the authorities' responses to the demonstrations in the Arab Spring of 2011, and in the Rif areas of the country beginning in 2016 and continuing into 2018, preserved order, but forever make it difficult for the King to claim that his administration would not resort to authoritarianism. Unrest during Rif protests was sparked largely by economic deprivation, although there were secondary factors that contributed to the demonstrations as well.[24]

From his first days as King, Morocco's Mohammed VI has been challenged from the left by those who want a more modern, and for some, a more secular democracy with greater state intervention. Yet, he also is challenged from the right by a Muslim Brotherhood who would like nothing better than to bypass many aspects of modernity in the political sphere while adopting many of the benefits of a modern economy for religious Islamic men. On the far right of the religious spectrum are those who believe only in a theocracy run by the clergy and see no role for a king, for women, or for democratic institutions. Others, with some allies in the Western international community, advocate for neoliberal economics with little regard for state intervention to provide a social safety net for citizens.

The King is also challenged by those who have historically occupied positions of power through their blood relations with, or social and business ties to, the sovereign on the throne. Many, though not all of these Makhzen, or advisers and associates of the King are accustomed to helping themselves to lucrative business enterprises that enrich themselves and their families rather than advance the economic development of the country.

For any ruler to thread his or her way through, such a bramble of oppositional forces while retaining legitimacy likely requires luck as well as skill. But there is no doubt that accelerating economic development and expanding access to economic activities help any leader gain the legitimacy to rule without resorting to violence.

Morocco's challenges in 1999 when King Mohammed VI ascended to the throne

1999 was a time of increasing globalization and liberalization in world history. IMF/World Bank high conditional structural adjustment programs were the norm, and neoliberal economic theories were championed by both international development banks and most Western donors. The Soviet Union had been dismantled for almost a decade, and socialist and communist development strategies were viewed as failed, costly, historic experiments. China was not yet a major force in international affairs. There simply was no coherent, persuasive alternative offered to the neoliberal economic policies that championed an unfettered market, and these policies were promoted by a wide array of Western powers and institutions.

The neoliberal structural adjustment policies as advocated by the IMF, the World Bank, and many Western donors are explained elsewhere but are noted here. In practice, they have included, for example, the devaluation of a country's currency; market pricing for all commodities, goods, and services; liberalization of trade beginning with steps to reduce tariffs; interest rate revisions; the promotion of treasury bills; an end to government control in favor of privatization; labor policy discipline to restrain wages (and inflation) and labor organizing; bureaucratic reorganization; increased capital investment; and the adoption of the concept of comparative advantage as a principle for making domestic economic policy as well as international production decisions.[25]

In the United States, President William (Bill) Clinton (1992–2000) argued that late industrializing states needed to create a welcoming and functioning business sector so that international investors (including US companies) could arrive and help jump start development while earning profits for themselves. "Engagement and Enlargement" was the name of the strategic doctrine later given to President Clinton's efforts to engage state leaders and their citizens around the world in international trade, international meetings, and cultural exchanges in order to bring all states into a democratic, capitalist global system.[26]

To promote his economic approach to development across sub-Saharan Africa, President Clinton announced on June 17, 1997, his "Partnership for Economic Growth and Opportunity in Africa."[27] This partnership, initiated two years before King Mohammed VI ascended his throne, included five major components: (1) enhanced trade programs and benefits to increase US-African trade and investment flows, targeted development aid, and commodity assistance; (2) technical assistance; (3) increased dialog with African countries through holding annual economic meetings at the cabinet/ministerial level with all reforming African nations; (4) financing and debt relief; and (5) continued US leadership in multilateral fora to promote the development and implementation of new initiatives that support private sector development, trade development, and institutional capacity building in African countries.[28]

Many agreed with President Clinton that trade and privatization would develop late industrializing states more effectively than had development assistance packages. Thus, "trade not aid" became a mantra for some. So too, did PPPs, a component of the "Third Way" espoused by President Clinton and the United Kingdom's Prime Minister, Tony Blair. PPPs relied heavily on private sector action but still required governments to offer public sector initiatives and supports for the private sector.

But, during the 1990s, there could also be seen increasing "pushback" by UN agencies and some donors (including both governments and international organizations) against the pristine policies of neoliberalism. This resistance called for a focus on poverty alleviation, decentralized decision-making, improving the status of women, and including historically disadvantaged populations in national development.[29]

Some critics at the UN, most famously Richard Jolly, Giovanni Andrea Cornia, and Frances Stewart, believed that pure neoliberal policies were not working and called for "adjustment with a human face." This was a clear reference to Czechoslovakia's Alexander Dubcek and his declared goal of creating "socialism with a human face" in his country when Dubcek believed that communist politics were not working.[30] Pointedly, the UN policy-makers pushed their analogy and titled their 1999 UN Human Development Report: "Globalization with a Human Face."

King Mohammed VI's preparations for leading Morocco

On July 23, 1999, when Morocco's new King, Mohammed VI, assumed his roles as Monarch and leader of his country, his choice from the many competing development strategies was likely derived from the programs that his father had already begun, as well as from his own experiences. Mohammed VI had done his primary studies in a religious school associated with the Palace. He completed his secondary studies in Morocco and then attended Mohammed V (named for his grandfather) University in Rabat to earn a degree in law, economics, and social sciences in 1985. He then did a postgraduate certificate in political science and a postgraduate diploma in law.

As a Prince, Mohammed VI traveled to various countries to meet with Heads of State – accompanying his father or going in place of his father. Mohammed VI learned a great deal about Europe's politics, economics, and security concerns from his EU assignment with Jacques Delors, the distinguished President of the European Commission and a former French Finance Minister. Mohammed VI also studied in France earning a Ph.D. with a doctorate focused on European–Moroccan trade. Having entered the Moroccan military prior to his European studies, Mohammed VI returned to Morocco to be appointed by his father as Coordinator of Services and Headquarters of the Royal Armed Forces. Later, he was promoted to Major General.

Yet, while Mohammed VI might have been a modern man of the world, in 1999, Morocco was in many ways an autocratic, precapitalist state. King Hassan II had been ruthless in centralizing power in the Monarchy as an institution; he destroyed the leaders of the political left and the religious right when either tried to assert themselves in Moroccan affairs. Nor did he share power with the center. The weapons of imprisonment and assassination were both utilized by Hassan II and his Interior Minister, Driss Basri. Neither the press nor the randomly and seldom called national elections were free or fair. Additionally, King Hassan II carefully monitored his public opinion, often seeking foreign affairs successes by which to rally national pride to support his leadership. He successfully dodged assassins and coups.

Economically, Hassan II was reported to have owned 20% of all agricultural land in Morocco, and his royal company controlled Morocco's lucrative phosphate mines. At the time of Hassan II's death, Morocco was the largest exporter of phosphates globally.[31] Yet even the King's enterprises were hurting because, in 1999, Morocco was enduring its second year of drought. Food was scarce, prices were high, and most Moroccans were hungry and uneasy with their lot. There was no reason for employers to employ Moroccans to work in fields that were barren. There was little food to purchase. Most Moroccans could see that the government had no viable plans; none for food and none for employment.

Other hardship for the average Moroccan came from the conditions of Morocco's IMF structural adjustment program. King Hassan was forced to borrow money and so adopt the structural adjustment policies due to the high costs of waging the Western Sahara military campaigns, the drought, lack of diversification and output of the economy, and the unstable costs of oil. The IMF plans required that Morocco, like other borrowers, devalue its currency (the Dirham), making it more expensive for Moroccans to pay for goods imported in internationally traded currencies. Additionally, the government was instructed to begin to privatize state-owned entities, to fire government workers in order to contain the budget, and to greatly reduce financial subsidies for food, health care, and education, also in order to curb the budget.

Simultaneously, bank interest rates were raised in the hopes of moderating the inflationary effects of the new IMF policies. That, of course, made it almost impossible for unemployed Moroccans to undertake any entrepreneurship activities because interest rates for borrowing to finance a new business were now prohibitive.

As a result, money was scarce, jobs were scarce, food was scarce, and bread prices rose. Healthcare was beyond reach, paying for education was a great luxury, and the cost of energy skyrocketed. Riots resulted and King Hassan II was forced partially to reinstate bread and energy subsidies. This cost the government much of the earnings it had gained by its privatization offering in the telecommunications sector.

King Hassan II was surrounded by a cohort of (almost exclusively) Moroccan men who benefitted from being relatives or friends of the King. Clientelism, patronage, and patriarchy comprised the template by which King Hassan II ruled Morocco. The Makhzen had deep stakes in the political and economic status quo. And of those Moroccans and foreigners who had resources and purchased Morocco's privatized companies, many were close to the Royals.

The average Moroccan life was a life of impoverishment. Eighty percent of the country's villages lacked both running water and electricity.[32] To allow some avenue for income for some Moroccans, it was reported that the King allowed the cultivation of Kif and hashish, which were then exported nine miles across the Mediterranean Sea to Spain and onto Europe. Further, with communications and transportation advances through globalization, Latin American drug lords focused on Tangier as a major transit point for hard drugs such as cocaine that came in from Latin America and went out across Europe.[33]

Years later, it was reported that the Makhzen themselves, perhaps even some Royals, engaged in the lucrative, illegal drug trade.[34] And over time, Spain was no longer the only entry point. In time, the drug boats could enter many ports across Europe. Much later, during the reign of Mohammed VI, some feared that the independent drug lords operating out of Morocco would become as much a security threat as were ISIS and other anti-governmental terrorists.[35] Additionally, the labor provided by the lucrative drug trade meant that thousands of Moroccans came to earn their livelihoods from, and therefore acquired loyalty to, Drug Barons.

Clearly, Morocco's new monarch, Mohammed VI was facing extraordinary challenges. When he assumed the throne, some dared to hope that the new King might adopt the Spanish model of democracy in which the monarch retained some powers over the military and played a role as Head of State while permitting a genuinely democratic parliament to contest, debate, and enact national laws. Others believed that Morocco's political parties were not yet ready for governance. One of the last political acts of King Hassan had been to allow the opposition parties to form a ruling bloc within the parliament. But King Hussein had retained decision-making authority, and it was clear that the Prime Minister was expected to work in partnership with the King.

One year after his ascension to the throne, Mohammed VI put into place a foundation that would make possible Morocco's first fair and free political party national elections; they would take place in 2002. Additionally, he immediately undertook steps to allow Moroccan women to play important roles in the political and public spheres as well as in Morocco's commercial and economic spheres.

The new King and his government introduced a six-month budget (July–December 2000) to increase revenues and development. The new King also extended many of the economic liberalization steps begun by his father. But everyone knew these would not suffice. In a globalizing world with accelerating communications, Moroccans could increasingly measure their country's lack of economic well-being against that of citizens in other countries. Thus, the new King began to "prime the pump" in an attempt to get money circulating in the economy. Taxes on property gains were abolished. Taxes on trade were reduced. Hotels were exempted from general taxes for five years, allowing the hotels to reduce rates in the hopes of attracting more tourists. It was announced that these measures would help to create 17,453 jobs. Additionally, King Mohammed VI flew to France and negotiated a debt conversion accord to reduce the country's debt. He also negotiated an FF100m aid package from the French government to be used to respond to the drought.[36]

But to attract investment and larger pools of tourists, Morocco needed to modernize its financial sector. King Hassan II had taken some steps to begin this process. Clearly, Mohammed VI hoped to accelerate the changes that were required. Chapter 2 explores the economic policies adopted by Mohammed VI to modernize the country's financial sector for it is this sector on which all others depend if development is to occur. Likewise, access to telecommunications is critical if a business is to function and if Moroccan citizens are to be able to contribute to economic efficiency and productivity. Chapter 3 analyzes the telecommunications sector. Similarly, the transport of goods and services and the energy sector are foundational to any developing country. Chapter 4 analyzes King Mohammed VI's prodigious efforts to modernize the transport sectors and also investigates efforts to expand exports in agriculture, pharmaceuticals, and textiles. As discussed in Chapter 8, these efforts did not just improve Morocco's economic standing but also helped the King to carry out economic statecraft to achieve some of Morocco's foreign policy goals.

Chapter 5 takes up the issue of Morocco's gamble to leapfrog in technology to allow solar, a renewable energy to play a major (though not exclusive) role in the country's energy economy. Chapter 6 looks at the impact that Moroccan corruption and lack of transparency likely has on the national economy and on citizen perceptions of national development.

Chapter 7 analyzes Morocco's tourism sector which has always been a source of foreign exchange and an engine of growth for the country.

Chapter 8 summarizes the book's overview of Morocco's economic choices in light of the development debates for late industrializing states. It argues that King Mohammed VI originally created a three-pronged development strategy that included (1) a focus on sectoral development, (2) an effort to leapfrog the technologies in which Morocco engaged, and (3) the adoption of what development researchers would call Morocco's own "variety of capitalism" in which neoliberal principles were ubiquitous but state interventions to guide development or intervene in the vagaries of the market to support some social justice concerns were also present. The final chapter also summarizes the strengths and weaknesses of Morocco's economy after two decades of rule (1999–2019) by Morocco's King Mohammed VI.

Notes

1 Although Mohammed VI studied in Morocco for his secondary and undergraduate work, he concluded graduate work in France writing a thesis on Moroccan-EU trade. He also worked for a brief period of time for the President of the EU Commission, Jacque Delors. From time to time, Mohammed VI also represented his father at international and regional gatherings. Mohammed VI was not insulated from global affairs.

2 United Nations, *Human Development Reports, 2018 Statistical Update.* (United Nations Development Programme) Retrieved from http://hdr.undp.org/en/2018-update.

3 The 2009 material was based on a study two years earlier in 2007 and reported in *Moroccan Business News* July 5, 2009. Retrieved January 21, 2019, from http://www.moroccobusinessnews.com/Content/Article.asp?idr=18&id=949.

4 Sandberg, E., & Binder, S. (2016). "The Moroccan Spring and King Mohammed VI's Economic Policy Agenda: Evaluating the First Dozen Years" in Mohsine El Ahmadi and Staurt Schaar, eds. *The Birth of the Arab Citizen and the Changing Middle East* (Northampton, MA: Interlink Publishing), p. 183.

5 See Maddy-Weitzman, B., & Zisenwine, D., eds. (2013). *Contemporary Morocco State, Politics and Society under Mohammed VI* (London and New York: Routledge), p. 3. Boukhars, A. (2010). *Politics in Morocco: Executive Monarchy and Enlightened Authoritarianism* (London and New York: Routledge).

6 Mohammed VI, Throne Speech July 29, 2017. Retrieved December 23, 2018, from https://www.moroccoworldnews.com/2017/07/224848/full-text-king-mohammed-vi-speech-throne-day/.

7 Mohammed VI, Throne Speech July 30, 2015. Retrieved December 23, 2018, from https://www.moroccoworldnews.com/2015/07/164318/full-text-of-king-mohammed-vis-speech-on-throne-day/.

8 Daadaoui, M. (2018, June 24). "The King's Dilemma in Morocco". Retrieved September 8, 2018, from http://www.maghreblog.com/2018/06/the-kings-dilemma-in-morocco.html.

9   Hancké, B. (2009). "Varieties of European Capitalism and Their Transformation" in Bob Hancké ed. *Debating the Varieties of Capitalism* (Oxford: Oxford University Press).
10 Stiglitz, J. E. (2011, August). "Rethinking Development Economics". *World Bank Research Observer* 26(2).
11 Ibid.
12 Ibid.
13 Khan, M. H. (2007, August) "Governance, Economic Growth and Development since the 1960s" (DESA Working Paper No. 54).
14 Ibid.
15 Ibid.
16 Ibid.
17 Sullivan, K. Eilperin, J., & Dennis, B. (2018, May 1). "Lobbyist Helped Arrange Scott Pruitt's $100,000 Trip to Morocco". *Washington Post*. Retrieved February 18, 2019, from https://www.washingtonpost.com/national/health-science/lobbyist-helped-broker-pruitts-100000-trip-to-morocco/2018/05/01/b2e20ee0-4d76-11e8-b725-92c89fe3ca4c_story.html?utm_term=.90f75e332f69.
18 For an account of the women's movement in Morocco up to the Spring of 2011, see Sandberg, E., & Aqertit, K. (2014). *Moroccan Women, Activists, and Gender Politics: An Institutional Analysis* (Lanham, MD: Lexington Books/Rowman & Littlefield).
19 Moroccan women may be found walking everywhere alone or in groups during the day. At night, it still is not advisable for a woman to walk alone.
20 United Nations Economic Commission for Europe, UNECE Policy for Gender Equality and the Empowerment of Women: Supporting the SDGs implementation in the UNECE region (2016–2020). Updated but no date given. Retrieved February 22, 2019, from http://www.unece.org/fileadmin/DAM/Gender/publications_and_papers/UNECE_Policy_on_GEEW_Final.pdf.
21 Amos, D. (2012, January 27). "In Morocco, Unemployment Can Be a Full-Time Job". Morning Edition National Public Radio (NPR). Retrieved August 15, 2018, from https://www.npr.org/2012/01/27/145860575/in-morocco-unemployment-can-be-a-full-time-job.
22 Slyomovics, S. (2005, April 4). "Morocco's Justice and Reconciliation Commission". Middle East Research and Information Project. Retrieved July 27, 2018, from https://www.merip.org/mero/mero040405.
23 Human Rights Watch, *World Report 2014: Morocco/Western Sahara Events of 2013*, p. 1.
24 The Rif Valley protests began after "a fishmonger was crushed inside a rubbish truck while trying to recover fish confiscated by police in the northern city of Al-Hoceima in October 2016." Eljechtimi, A. (2018, July 15). "Tens of Thousands Protest in Morocco over Jailed Rif Activists." *Reuters*. Retrieved February 22, 2019, from https://www.reuters.com/article/us-morocco-protests-idUSKBN1K50R0. Secondary factors for the escalation of the protests included the unwillingness of former Prime Minister Abdelilah Benkirane, the former leader of the Party of Justice and Democracy (PJD), to assist in calming the protesters. Political analysts contend that King Mohammed VI earlier had circumvented Benkirane (whose party was having difficulty forming a coalition with other parties in Parliament in order to claim leadership), by not reappointing him as Prime Minister when it was clear he was becoming a national hero to many and a locus of power that might one day challenge the King. Or perhaps, it was because Benkirane was a hindrance to modern development or a Prime Minister that other parties could not work with. Saadeddine Othmani, who had served as Morocco's Minister of Foreign Affairs for the PJD government, was elevated to Prime Minister. Protests continued on the Rif when protest leaders were sentenced to 20 years in prison.

25 Sandberg, E. (1995, November). *The Impact of the International Monetary Fund's Structural Adjustment Program on the Agricultural Sector in Zambia 1985.* Case Study #213, Pew Charitable Trusts, Institute for the Study of Diplomacy, Georgetown University (60 pages).
26 Clinton, W. J. (1996). *A National Security Strategy of Engagement and Enlargement 1995–1996.* (San Francisco, CA: Brassey's).
27 *A Comprehensive Trade and Development Policy for the Countries of Africa.* A Report Submitted by the President of the United States to Congress the Third of Five Annual Reports December 1997.
28 Ibid.
29 In Morocco, historically disadvantaged communities would include the Berber communities.
30 Unfortunately, Dubcek's deviation from adherence to strict Soviet policies led to the Soviet/Warsaw Pact invasion of Czechoslovakia in 1968.
31 *Africa Research Bulletin*, (1999, July 1) 36(7), 13604.
32 Ibid.
33 Ketterer, J. (2001, Spring). "Networks of Discontent in Northern Morocco". *Middle East Research,* 31(218). Downloaded March 5, 2018.
34 "A Tanger, deux milles jeunes emeutiers ont affronte les forces de l'ordre," *Le Monde* June 7, 1996.
35 Ketterer, J. "Networks of Discontent in Northern Morocco". op. cit.
36 The components of Mohammed VI's first budget detailed in the paragraph above are reported in (2000). *African Research Bulletin*, 2000 37(3), 14289.

2 Modernizing Morocco's strategies to manage capital and professionalizing the country's financial sector officials

Economic development requires any state's officials to oversee effective financial sustainability in their country. Demonstrating judicious economic policies guards against capital flight and helps citizens and foreigners risk investment in productive activities or make purchases in the local market. Government officials must support their economy directly and indirectly, as well as convince both domestic and foreign sources of capital to underwrite new and expanding businesses. State officials also must protect their country's economy from external financial shocks. Obviously, capital alone will not develop or modernize any state. But the management of capital remains central to any country's development process.

This chapter first provides a brief summary of the findings of our analysis of Morocco's development of its financial sector under King Mohammed VI during the past 20 years. It then identifies the reasons for Morocco's lack of capital when King Mohammed VI inherited the throne from his father Hassan II. The chapter then analyzes King Mohammed VI's efforts to professionalize Morocco's banking sector, attract foreign (including expatriate) investment and financial support, and adopt "participatory banking" practices (Morocco's counterpart to Islamic banking practices). It also notes Morocco's creation of the Casablanca Finance City Authority (CFCA) and the country's new initiatives to fund small- and medium-sized enterprises. The chapter concludes with an analysis of Morocco's successes of its financial sector as well as its continuing needs.

A brief summary of our analysis of King Mohammed VI's financial sector

From the traditional standards by which financial sectors are managed, Morocco's improvement in its financial sector, an early major focus of King Mohammed VI, is a stunning success, though there is still work to be done. New important regulations were enacted that protected investors, intellectual property rights, and provided support for major projects. Moroccan professionals in this sector underwent training and can now conduct sophisticated banking and business transactions. The number of Moroccans who utilize formal banking practices has also increased.

For Moroccans of modest means, however, there remain barriers to obtaining credit for housing and for small- and medium-sized businesses. This disparity contributes to the enduring perception that Morocco's economic policies benefit the state itself through new tax revenues, provide new investment opportunities for those already economically advantaged, and create demonstration projects of modern development to impress foreigners. For Morocco's lower middle class and its poor, little has changed in their ability to access credit or jobs over the past 20 years, despite various announcements from time to time by Moroccan leaders regarding their intent to address these issues. Recently, in 2018, the King and his advisers announced new initiatives to address some of the economic concerns of Morocco's most disadvantaged. So, we can state that in the past 20 years, under the leadership of King Mohammed VI, Morocco has modernized its financial sector significantly, and we anticipate it will continue the modernization of this sector. Its task now is to expand the scope of those who benefit from this sector. If there is a political will to match the sector's new technical abilities with programs to address those who are historically disadvantaged, then the next ten years should bring successes in this sector that benefit all Moroccans.

Morocco's record of managing capital under Hassan II, prior to the ascension of Mohammed VI

Control of the capital operating within a late industrializing state has long been a goal of the leaders of such states. Additionally, state investment into national infrastructure is an important prerequisite for attracting any capital investments – foreign or domestic – in new productive endeavors. Thus, raising capital and controlling its allocation, as well as investing in new infrastructure projects, were key goals for King Hassan II, though in his 38 years of reign he never achieved the successes that his son, Mohammed VI, was able to secure. In the 1970s, the second decade of King Hassan's reign, four major factors influenced Morocco's ability to control and raise capital. Then, in subsequent years, four additional factors affected Morocco's financial abilities beyond those core four of the 1970s.

First, in a parallel action to that taken by many other late industrializing states, King Hassan II instituted a policy of "Moroccanization" (in March 1973), requiring that all major companies operating in the country have 51% ownership by Moroccan citizens. This measure brought large portions of the economy under the purview of the King and those he favored. It added to the King's and the Makhzen's earlier initiatives to acquire foreign-owned agricultural land, which King Hassan had originally intimated would largely be made available for small holder production.

Moroccanization of the manufacturing and industrial sectors meant that foreign companies had to scramble to find Moroccan partners. As Greg White's research on this policy noted, the King also used Moroccanization politically to create a "factional stalemate within the elite" by offering commercial jobs in return for support among Morocco's competing actors who were vying for both political and economic power.[1] Thus, the use of new capital opportunities provided the King with political quiescence as well as domestic participation in the country's economic activities. And as White and others have noted, following several coup attempts in the early 1970s, and with the military's loyalty suspect, King Hassan had to find new ways to give important leaders a stake in Morocco's system.

There is little doubt that Moroccanization was politically useful. But unfortunately the economic policies of Moroccanization ultimately deterred international investment in Morocco because some foreign corporate owners who might have contemplated initiating new business endeavors in Morocco did not care to share a major portion of their businesses or technologies with Moroccans. Those foreigners who already had sunken capital costs into Morocco were the ones from whom King Hassan and his associates profited. In 1993, six years before Hassan II died, the Moroccanization law was repealed and new legislation was passed so that foreign companies were allowed to repatriate 100% of their capital out of country.

Other factors also helped to provide Morocco with much-needed capital. The 1970s saw significant increases in the commodity price of phosphates, a major export of Morocco. Morocco was the third largest global producer of phosphates during this decade. Thus, the government was soon earning increased revenues and, in turn, state investment within Morocco rose dramatically hitting its highest level in 1978.[2] According to John Waterbury, Alan Richards, and Gregory White, between 1970 and 1976, the number of public sector firms in Morocco increased from 137 to 238 as King Hassan used both Moroccanization and phosphates to deepen and expand Morocco's bourgeoisie and support its Makhzen.[3] But much of Morocco's investment was dependent upon, loans from the Office Cherifien des Phosphates (OCP) whose Director was appointed by the King.[4] By the end of the 1970s, almost any business needing capital had to approach the King's Director for loans. And because Morocco lacked a modern banking sector, decisions were frequently based on political, not economic, considerations. Melani Claire Cammett has documented, building on earlier work by John Waterbury and Abdelkader Berrada, how Moroccan business families with longstanding external business ties of their own came to understand that, in the personalized political economy of King Hassan II, acquiring government positions and influencing government policies benefitted their businesses.[5] Soon the lines separating business elites and state officials were blurred.[6]

Moroccan state leaders anticipated continued phosphate revenues to buoy the economy. But in 1979, the Organization of the Petroleum

Exporting Countries (OPEC)'s oil price increases caused major financial burdens for all states and this affected Morocco in ways known as the "scissors effect." First all countries, including Morocco, had to pay more for energy. Energy is used in both the production and the transport of all goods. Paying more for energy meant spending less on other goods and services and it meant that the costs of goods that were produced rose. With a rise in prices of produced goods, consumers of goods cut back in their spending. Demand decreased and inventories stockpiled. This occurred in both Morocco and in the countries to which Morocco traditionally exported. Phosphate prices declined as demand declined globally in the face of less productivity due to higher energy prices. But Morocco continued to need imports – now more costly because the energy costs to produce them had increased. But the country had less revenue. So, Morocco was soon overspending and the country's debt began to climb. OPEC energy price increases thus comprise a significant third factor affecting Morocco's capital and debt profile after Moroccanization and phosphates. OPEC raised its prices significantly in both 1973 and 1979. Both initiatives took a toll on Morocco's economy.[7]

The fourth factor during King Hassan's reign throughout the 1970s that made investment in the country's economy difficult was the costs of Morocco's Western Sahara war. The Western Sahara war undermined Morocco's ability to finance its own budget and also less capital was available to invest in sustainable economic activities. In 1975, King Hassan led a long march of over 300,000 Moroccans to the Western Saharan territory in order to demonstrate the depth of the Moroccan people's belief in their claim to the Western Sahara as part of the nation's sovereign territory. The Polisario Front, the military arm of the Sahrawi separatist movement had declared the Western Sahara an independent state, named the Sahrawi Arab Democratic Republic. The Polisario Front maintained that Western Sahara had never been a part of Morocco, and that following Spain's withdrawal from the area, it should be an independent state with the Front serving as the new country's government. The Polisario Front was supported by Morocco's neighbor, Algeria. Thus, from 1975 to 1991, the government of Morocco spent large sums on a war of secession in the Western Sahara before the United Nations brokered a peace beginning on September 6, 1991.

Politically, King Hassan's campaign to govern the Western Sahara proved to be wildly popular among Moroccan citizens during the 1970s and 1980s. But if King Hassan had been expecting a quick war and access to the underground riches (phosphate, uranium, and oil) of the Western Sahara, he was mistaken. The Western Saharan war cost Moroccans dearly. Future costs and benefits, however, remain unclear because many countries across Africa and in other regions have retreated from actively supporting the Polisario Front. In January 2019, for example, despite major lobbying from the Polisario and the government of Algeria to block any agreement, the European Union (EU) and Morocco concluded an agriculture and fishing deal that Morocco had long sought. The Polisario objected and claimed the fish and waters in part of those agreements belonged to their declared state. But the Europeans, like many African states who now are investigating business deals with Morocco, were ready to do business with Morocco and let the United Nations and other international bodies deal with the Western Sahara issue.

In the early 1980s and 1990s, additional factors contextualized Morocco's ability to control its capital and to finance its own development. In the early 1980s, to pay its debts and run its government, Morocco borrowed heavily from the Bretton Woods Institutions (BWIs) and began to implement the requisite Structural Adjustment Programs (SAPs) required by the World Bank and the International Monetary Fund (IMF) in exchange for the financial loans they provided. The Independent Evaluation Group (IEG) – a professional group that "evaluates the development effectiveness of the World Bank Group" while operating independently and reporting only to the Executive Board of the World Bank Group – identifies 1983 as the turning point in World Bank–Morocco relations.[8]

King Hassan's economic measures adopted under the SAP were typical for indebted countries. In accordance with the SAP, Hassan II began the process of liberalizing foreign trade and investment as well as privatizing Moroccan businesses. King Hassan also embraced the principles of financial discipline required by the conditions of Morocco's loans from the BWIs.

King Hassan initiated austerity measures that sharply reduced subsidies for food staples, laid off workers, and restricted wage increases for most remaining government-employed workers.[9] And Hassan began the process of privatizing several state-led sectors of Morocco's economy. Many of the new private owners who benefited from the privatization sales were individuals favored by the King; family members, associates, and friends were able secure former state enterprises to own and operate in the private sector.

The austerity measures that removed subsidies and resulted in an increase in prices for food and other goods led to major protests and demonstrations. Some of Morocco's political party leaders and some union leaders who opposed the austerity policies abandoned their quiescence and began speaking in the public realm, challenging the new policies. The protests grew. But Hassan's police shot at the crowds that demonstrated and the police killed hundreds while many union and political leaders were arrested and "disappeared" into Morocco's notorious prisons.[10] This was not the first time that Hassan had used brutal force to silence disagreement but in the 1980s, it became clear that the legitimacy of the monarchy in Morocco was shaken. It was a steep price to pay in order for Morocco to finance its budget through BWI loans, but Hassan could find no other way to finance the Kingdom.

A fifth factor also greatly affected the health of the Moroccan economy and the financial situation of Morocco's citizens during the reign of Hassan II. European officials guarded their Common Agricultural Policy (CAP) by limiting Maghreb country exports to Europe. The CAP not only restricted importation of certain goods into Europe that European members of the then European Economic Community (EEC) (later absorbed into the EU) produced but also subsidized EU farmers so that they could sell their products below world market prices and compete successfully with Moroccan and other late industrializing state producers across international markets.

The economic recession of the 1980s also affected the finances of late industrializing states like Morocco. Difficult economic times in the Western advanced industrialized countries undercut Morocco's anticipated investment by foreigners as well as slowed any exports it had hoped to ship to Europe. This is because the demand structure in Europe and elsewhere had shrunk during this global recession that had begun in the 1970s and stubbornly continued into the 1980s.

Then in the early 1990s, the EEC expanded to include Greece, Spain, and Portugal followed by a number of Eastern European states. This critically hurt Moroccan farmers because they now had to compete with even more European farmers who produced many of the same agricultural products that Moroccan farmers produced.[11] These new producers were accorded all the protections that earlier European producers claimed as members. Morocco had hoped to be allowed to join the EEC and later the EU when the EU was launched in 1993, but over the decades, Moroccan inquiries and applications for entry continued to be rebuffed by the European states.

Thus when Mohammed VI ascended to the throne in 1999, he inherited a capital resource and revenue system that was largely unstable and unavailable to most Moroccans. He had little room in which to maneuver in his initial years of governing. Likewise, the process of privatization had been uneven. And Moroccan business elites were accustomed to protections offered by the King and their connections across the government. Business elites focused less on professionalizing their staff or improving their technologies, than on securing and becoming integrated into the multiple networks of state leaders.

In 1999, at the time of the royal transition, what revenues Morocco earned in foreign exchange came mainly from phosphates, tourism (mostly from Europe and especially from France), from remittances (funds sent back to families and to businesses in Morocco from those Moroccans who had gone abroad to seek a better life), and also from agricultural exports. But each of these four sources of Morocco's income was, in turn, reliant on external forces to sustain it.

Morocco continued to export phosphates, but a number of additional countries also began exporting the commodity and the global economy would need to continue expanding if phosphate revenues were to remain steady and finance Morocco's economy. When discretionary incomes rose internationally, tourists (mainly from Europe) were encouraged to visit Morocco. Good will from Moroccan expatriates toward Moroccans at home encouraged remittances. But it also was the good will toward Moroccan expatriates in their adopted countries as well as a strong economy in their adopted countries that provided the sense of security that encouraged expatriated Moroccans to send resources home. Adequate rain and sun were obvious factors influencing the levels of Moroccan agriculture production both for export and for domestic consumption, as were the changing policies of European states and the new EU.

It was no wonder that a joint mission by the World Bank and IMF in 2002, three years after Mohammed VI assumed the throne, found that "Morocco's macroeconomic policies and practices as a whole tend to err more on the side of the concerns of protecting the economy from external shocks."[12] Morocco certainly was vulnerable to international economic factors and also to its large and powerful neighbors to the north, in the EU. As first Peter Katzenstein argued, and as Gregory White demonstrated with regard to Morocco, small middle-income countries like Morocco had been integrated into the economies of their former colonizers and their economic ties continued into the post-independence era.[13] But the routinized production policies of the newly independent states yielded poor results for the former colony. The former colonial exporters had market niches in their former colonial powers and so the former colonies were dependent on sales in that country. Second, post-independent states generally do not invest in the economies of scale in production that would meet their own domestic needs and so continue to have to import goods and services.[14] Finally, Morocco, like other such countries, did not give adequate attention to diversifying its production.[15] With its eggs largely in the European basket for both exports and imports, when Mohammed VI assumed the throne, Morocco remained extraordinarily vulnerable to French and other European countries' changing economic conditions and to an overreliance on agriculture which, in turn, was dependent on good rains in Morocco and policies and weather in European states.

The next section of this chapter analyzes the beginnings of the professionalization of human capital in the financial sector. It also analyzes the expansion and upgrade of the financial sector by Mohammed VI and his ministers that has proved so necessary for the sector to play a foundational role for development across the country.

The mobilization of domestic capital and the professionalization of Morocco's banking sector

The mobilization of capital is critical for any new economic endeavors and for any economic development to take place. But capital cannot simply be secured; it must be managed by professional financial actors who in effect work at the hub of a country's productive activity. In the early years of Mohammed VI's reign, it was clear that civil servants and decision-makers needed to upgrade their professional skills.

In 2001, just two years after the change in the Monarchy (in 1999), Moroccan government officials were required to participate in workshops and trainings that promoted public sector reforms and introduced "results-based budgeting and management" practices.[16] While such an initiative was important for all sectors of the country, it was especially important for the financial and banking sectors. Foreign investors would not be attracted to invest in Morocco unless they were assured that the finance sector allowed for transparency and also practiced competent record keeping. Moreover, plans for economic development, led by the private sector or through public/private partnerships, were framed through capital support. Professionalizing the financial sector was foundational to expanding economic development.

A 2003 IMF review and report on Morocco's financial system called for more openness but, interestingly, it also advised that the Moroccan government create a monetary policy that allowed it to intervene in the country's economy in order to target and manage price stability. The same 2003 IMF report noted that two of Morocco's state banks were insolvent and that there was an evident need to restructure Morocco's financial institutions.[17]

At the time of King Mohammed VI's accession to the throne, Morocco's financial sector was controlled by the state and lacked easy foreign exchange conversion, though Hassan II had put in place some policies to begin the liberalization of the financial sector after 1993. Between 1999 and 2019, however, during the reign of Mohammed VI, Morocco successfully reorganized its banking sector and also the role of banks in its development strategies.

Morocco's banking services are now available to over 60% of its population. In 2018 there were:

> 19 banks operating in Morocco as well as seven offshore institutions. In addition, there are 34 non-banking financial institutions, including 16 consumer credit specialists, 13 microcredit lenders and six leasing companies in Morocco. The sector is dominated by locally owned banks, which account for 82.3% of industry assets.[18]

It should be noted, however, that as of June 2016, the top three banks in Morocco accounted for 65.6% of the country's total banking assets.[19] It also needs to be noted that while over 60% of the country has access to banking services, less than 30% of Moroccan citizens hold bank accounts. Additionally, there is a double-digit gender gap between male and female holders of Moroccan bank accounts.

But Morocco's financial sector has been fundamentally transformed and such an improvement in any sector does not occur overnight. New practices can take years before they become part of the standard operating procedures of state and private institutions. Thus, Morocco's financial and banking systems are noteworthy for having achieved high standards of excellent performance over the past 20 years. The need now is for Morocco's financial institutions to reach and support all Moroccans, not just the most economically active citizens.

In the 12 years between 1999 and 2011, Morocco's banking institutions were strengthened and its new business regulatory practices made the country attractive, especially to large-scale investors. Additionally, foreign banks were permitted and encouraged to locate and do business in Morocco. By 2010, only 27% of Morocco's banking sector was owned by the state.[20] Growth in credit from many sources resulted and both domestic and international investment soared.

It followed that Morocco's international monetary ratings saw improvement as well. Standard and Poor's raised Morocco's foreign currency creditworthiness to BBB– (its lowest investment grade) and Morocco's local currency achieved a BBB+ in March 2010. Additionally, Fitch rated Morocco as "stable," which upgraded Moroccan financial instruments to "investment grade," thus attracting new buyers and capital from international markets.[21] Additionally, Morocco's new, improved capital markets showed the most diversity in their region, offering banking, equity, and bonds. Rated as 22 in the MSCI Emerging Markets Index, Morocco climbed onto "the radar screen of not only local but also international institutional investors."[22] In just one decade, Morocco's banking sector was modernized in ways that integrated it into the international political economy. In fact, in 2010, the Moroccan bank, Attijariwafa, received the coveted award, "African Bank of the Year" that is announced annually at the IMF/World Bank meetings. Such recognition was a stunning result from efforts in just one decade.

One modern financial instrument that King Mohammed VI inherited was Morocco's stock exchange, the Casablanca Stock Exchange founded in 1929. Morocco has operated a modern stock market since 1993 when it renamed the market the Société de Bourse des Valeurs de Casablanca (SBVC) and identified a private company whose capital is jointly owned by various brokerage firms to run it.[23] In 2000, the SBVC was renamed the Casablanca Stock Exchange and it signaled a new era for Morocco's equity market. Although Morocco's stock market was small, by 2013, it was Africa's fourth largest capitalized equity market.[24] In 2013, South Africa had a stock market with the greatest equity at $970.5 billion in assets, followed by Namibia at $136.9 billion, and then Nigeria at $114.2 billion.[25] Then, there is a large drop in the equity of other countries' stock markets. And Morocco tops the list of the second group; Morocco's stock market was capitalized at $54.8 billion, Egypt at $54.3 billion (a decline due in large measure to its political uncertainties), and then another sharp drop to $28.2 billion for Ghana and $20.6 billion for Kenya.[26] Other African states' equity markets for whom there is information, ranged from single digits to lower double digits.[27]

Morocco's stock market capitalization would seesaw over the next few years, but it remained in the realm of $50 plus billion. And, despite the Moroccan Spring, Morocco was recognized with the award of "African County of the Future" and announced to be the "best investment destination in Africa" in 2011–2012 by the foreign direct investment (FDI) intelligence division of the *Financial Times*.[28]

Despite Morocco's international success, domestic critics claim that during this period there was not enough access to credit for the average Moroccan. And so even if Morocco's King and his advisers have been careful to modernize institutionally in ways that provide a firm foundation for future investment benefits, this does not take away the sting of the slow economic development that most Moroccans endure presently. Additionally, some Moroccans believe that they have been denied access to credit and economic development due to widespread corruption across Moroccan society. Such corruption is perceived to be with collaboration from the top. This makes the sting of having been left behind in Morocco's developing path more difficult to accept.

In terms of categorizing Morocco's program of development in the financial sector, King Mohammed VI and his governments chose to pursue the neoliberal strategies for modernizing the economy that had begun during the reign of his father, Hassan II. But Mohammed VI did so with an eye to the limits of what he could do in the short term in Morocco. For example, instead of adopting strict free-market currency practices, Morocco pegged its foreign exchange rate to a basket of currencies from its important trading partners, a practice that was common among other late industrializing states and had become acceptable to the BWIs. Partially, as a result of this, as well as through intervention in its currency markets, and the continuation of modest subsidies (discussed below), Morocco avoided a huge devaluation of its currency all at once and the kind of economic shocks experienced by other countries. Morocco's inflation rates over the past decade have been low for a late industrializing country. A decade into Mohammed VI's reign, Morocco's inflation declined "from 3.9% in 2008 to 1% in 2009, a level Morocco maintained during 2010 and 2011."[29]

Additionally, King Mohammed VI and his advisors have not been afraid to run a national deficit when needed. Opinions on incurring such a deficit vary. Austerity hawks oppose such a practice. Those who believe government must act to provide for the general welfare in times of economic downturn believe that some government deficit spending is within the realm of prudent fiscal management. Morocco largely has been able to balance its spending against its income to avoid excessive long-term compounding debt, even if it operates at a deficit.

Morocco's current account deficit in 2010 was more than 4% of its GDP, and the IMF estimated that it could double in 2011, to 8.9% of GDP.

However, King Mohammed VI insisted on continuing to subsidize food and energy prices for Moroccan citizens despite a November 2011 IMF communication that warned about the extent of debt that would result from such actions. The IMF communication noted that "Maintaining prices for certain food products and fuel unchanged in the context of rising international commodity prices, will require spending...of about 5½% of GDP in 2011."[30]

However, the King's commitment to providing a social safety net for Moroccan citizens and finding ways to advance human development had been highlighted in his May18, 2005 speech in which he launched Morocco's National Initiative for Human Development. According to the Moroccan government's official website, in this speech, the King committed himself to

> attack the social deficit by making the basic social services more accessible, promote activities likely to create employment opportunities and stable incomes, adopt an imaginative action towards the informal sector, and help people suffering vulnerability and those with specific needs.[31]

The speech was given after the King and his advisers had time to contemplate the causes of the horrific bombings of Casablanca in 2003 by Moroccan youth who had been recruited to perform terrorist attacks.

Thus, while King Mohammed VI committed himself to modernizing foundational sectors in the economy such as finance, he also walked a fine line in order to maintain a social safety net – a net that proved too great for some international BWI officials, but too little for many Moroccan citizens who were struggling economically. The range of Morocco's current account deficit to GDP was recorded as follows:

Morocco's Current Account Deficit to GDP

2009	2010	2011	2012	2013	2014	2015	2016	2017	2018
5.4	4.4	7.6	9.3	7.6	5.7	2.2	4.4	4	

Source 2009–2017: Trading Economics: https://tradingeconomics.com/morocco/current-account-to-gdp. (Note that 2017 is a rounded estimate and was later recorded at 3.6%.)

In addition to professionalizing the finance sector by improving the skills and working habits of its employees, and of identifying the range in which Morocco would run a deficit, another area of success for Mohammed VI's efforts to modernize the country's financial sector included Morocco's tax officials who identified the goals of broadening the tax system while lowering taxes. More taxes would mean more money was available for financing domestic investment.

By 2007, corporate tax rates were set in the 30% plus range but could easily be reduced to 28% through compliance with incentive schemes and could be eliminated for five-year holidays under compliance with other conditions.[32] On paper, the tax system was standardized so that it was hoped that the situation of a company or individual, not whom they or their corporate officers knew, would dictate their tax rates. By 2011, the Director General of MedZ Sourcing, Abderrafie Hanouf, noted that within Morocco's creatively designed "offshore sector" business parks, tax rates could be reduced from 38% to 20% in the first five years of a company's operation.[33]

However, as the government began in 2019 to try to capture those who were avoiding taxes in their day-to-day operations, by identifying those who were not conducting business through transparent electronic means, Morocco's merchants pushed back. In January 2019, Article 145 of the General Code of Taxes on electronic billing and the use of the business identification number went into effect. The law stated that merchants were required to use electronic billing for all commercial transactions.

In response, on January 3, 2019, Casablanca wholesalers closed their businesses in protest. Other parts of the country saw protests as well. On January 17, 2019, many Rabat merchants also went on strike. Moroccan residents found there were few places in which they could purchase products unless they had transportation to the large megastores.

The law required that merchants purchase electronic devices that are compatible with in-putting data into Morocco's national tax agency's files and that they use electronic billing for their transactions. But the merchants' protests forced Moroccan officials to back down. The implementation of the law was scrapped in its first month.[34]

In sum, under the leadership of King Mohammed VI, the last dozen years have seen a much-needed modernization of the financial sector in Morocco though work remains. In fact, by 2008, Morocco was ranked 89th in the world's "soundest financial systems" ahead of states with much larger economies such as Japan (93rd), Russia (107th), China (108th), and Turkey (114th).[35] Morocco had privatized some of its public banks. It had modernized its payment system, and it had passed anti-money laundering and anti-terrorist finance laws. Additionally, Morocco's Conseil Déontologique des Valeurs Mobilières (CDVM), Morocco's ethics council for its securities was given important powers to regulate securities.

However, in 2008, the IMF noted that "only 37% of the population has a bank account, fewer than 50,000 persons hold shares, and insurance premia are less than USD 65 per capita."[36] In response to this situation and cognizant of the need to mobilize domestic savings, Mohammed VI's government took action to create a banking subsidiary of its national postal system. The new subsidiary, Al-Barid Bank (ABB), used

> the post office's extensive rural infrastructure to provide loans, cash transfers, ATMs and other credit facilities. ABB has also introduced

a mobile payments system, available to both clients and non-account holders, and smaller outlets with more flexible opening hours that offer cash transfers.[37]

In just four years, Moroccan citizens who could access banking services increased from 34% (sic: a lower figure than the IMF figure noted previously) to 62% and between 400,000 and 500,000 accounts per year were activated.[38] By the end of 2014, Al-Barid could boast that it held accounts for about 16% of Morocco's population.[39] And the Moroccan government rightly noted proudly that many of these accounts were in rural areas. The use of postal office branches for financial transactions could be found in various European states, but it was to Moroccan leaders' credit that they instituted such an infrastructure for their own citizens and accomplished it so quickly.

Al-Barid first partnered with Société de Financement d'Achats à Crédit so that unlike the Postal Service, it could offer loans. Al-Barid also formed an agreement with Morocco's social security agency for direct deposits.[40] Then, in 2011, Al-Barid entered into a partnership with MoneyGram International, a company that transfers money internationally, that opened its first office in Morocco in 1998. With the new partnership, MoneyGram International extended its presence in Morocco by operating in all of Al-Barid's 1,800 locations that existed in 2011 and so totaling MoneyGram International's presence at over 5,000 locations across Morocco.[41]

Then, Al-Barid partnered with Eurogiro (a multi-platform payment network) and it soon handled almost 80% of Morocco's domestic transfers.[42] With easier procedures for money transfers and a multitude of new locations in which to transfer funds, Al-Barid's international remittances coming into Morocco soared. Al-Barid was designated as an independent entity and continued in 2018 to increase its activities.

While many see remittances as a positive financial inflow to assist family members, some worry that remittances may create a culture of dependency for its recipients or add to inflationary pressures for families that do not receive remittances. Additionally, because many of Morocco's migrants are males and some have high levels of education, remittances have been seen, by some, as an indicator of the brain drain from a country.[43] If a person has emigrated and is doing well enough to send back remittances, the birth country should have found a way to retain that person argue those who see remittances as part of the brain drain. Others, however, argue that more attention needs to be given to the positive benefits of remittances such as helping family members to start small enterprises.

Drawing on the work of many recent studies in disparate academic fields, Andrea Gallina argues that remittances counter the export of capital from Morocco and also play an important role in developing the human capital of Moroccan citizens.[44] The money sent back to Morocco often pays for education, healthcare, and contributes to the nourishment of Moroccan individuals who form the work force in Morocco.[45] Further in 2008, Mohamed

Berriane and Mohamed Aderghal concluded a comprehensive study of all aspects of Moroccan migration and noted that, "remittances now provide between 8 and 9% of the country's GDP." [46] In 2015, Morocco's remittances brought $6.4 billion into Morocco.[47] In 2017, remittances to Morocco accounted for 6.79% of GDP.[48] The top ten countries from which remittances came into Morocco in the final years of Mohammed VI's first two decades of reign are as follows: France, Spain, Italy, Belgium, the Netherlands, Israel, Germany, the United States, Canada, and the United Kingdom.[49] Clearly, such payments are important to Moroccans who did not leave the country as such inflows of capital support Morocco's social safety net, but they also make available some start-up capital for those who hope to undertake new enterprises.

In 1990, King Hassan had created a Ministry of Moroccan Residents Abroad largely to advocate on their behalf in their new home countries. On assuming the throne, King Mohammed VI creatively responded to the challenge of his diaspora community. In 2003, the King created a new commission on the human rights of immigrants and in 2006 began consultations with leaders in Morocco's diaspora community to create in 2008 the *Conseil Supérieur de la Communauté Marocaine à l'Etranger* (CSCME), the High-Level Council for the Moroccan Community living Abroad (composed of 37 members appointed by the King). Efforts were made to ease holiday returns for offshore Moroccans and to make the transfers of remittances easier as well. Additionally, partnerships in host countries have assisted Moroccan officials with offering workshops concerning investment opportunities in Morocco and concerning advice on how to negotiate the processes for investing in Morocco. Though the King's efforts have been derided by some critics, the King's outreach to Moroccans abroad has dramatically increased remittances, persuaded some skilled Moroccans to return home, and also laid the ground work for additional investment in Morocco.

The Moroccan situation with regards to migrants is a difficult one that we do not discuss in detail in this study. In recent years, Morocco has become a destination for many sub-Saharan migrants coming to Morocco and hoping to pass through to Europe or deciding to try to stay in Morocco. Caring for this group has been expensive. Additionally, not all Moroccans who leave Morocco are searching for economic improvement. Moroccan women have fled brutal arranged marriages in which they had no voice. Some Moroccans have married non-Moroccans and emigrated. But for this study, it is important to understand that for those Moroccans who emigrated and send remittances back to their family, remittances form one element of Morocco's financial profile.

Another success for Morocco in managing its financial sector was the actions of Morocco's Central Bank (Bank Al Maghrib) that guided the financial sector through the 2008 crisis. In 2008, Morocco, like most countries around the world, suffered an increase in non-performing loans. In fact, most of Morocco's economy suffered as a result of the 2008 Western economic crisis, but fortunately its financial sector did not suffer greatly. The IMF noted that this was "because Moroccan external debt is low and has long maturities, and macroeconomic policies have been strengthened in recent years."[50] This was quite a change *in just six years* from the observations of the joint IMF World Bank mission in 2002 quoted in the beginning of this chapter.

And in addition to securing FDI from abroad, Morocco was exporting its own currency as an investor of FDI to other African states. This phenomenon was not just good business, it was an important component of Morocco's economic statecraft to raise Morocco's standing in the region.[51] As of May 2017, Morocco's "Attijariwafa Bank, for example, operates in 13 Sub-Saharan countries and BMCE has a network of 19 franchises in the region."[52] However, such operations create a drag on Morocco's own development. As Fitch ratings in London has noted,

> Moroccan banks that establish or acquire banks in markets with lower sovereign ratings are exposed to the large portfolios of local government bonds that these subsidiaries will typically hold. In most African markets, domestic sovereign bonds are rated several notches lower than Moroccan sovereign bonds (BBB−). Operating environments are also typically more risky, exposing banks to greater asset risk, and regulatory standards may be less developed than they are in Morocco.[53]

In response to the increases in currency flows into and out from Morocco, the country's officials have learned to pay close attention to foreign currency exchange rate practices. From 1998 until January 15, 2018, IMF and World Bank officials pressed the Moroccan government to abandon all foreign exchange control policies. But the Moroccan leaders knew that any quick devaluations and the resulting economic shocks would bring more inflation to Moroccan citizens who purchase many goods that are produced abroad (or to those who had to travel abroad). And, as the cost of imports rose, inflation would soon spread across the economy. Then, most likely, as in other countries, social unrest would follow. So, Mohammed VI and his economic advisers adopted other BWI policies but stalled on the requests for deep devaluations. Instead, they creatively crafted their own currency policies for Morocco's currency, the Dirham.

Morocco's leaders waited until a sizeable middle class had developed over time and waited for a year of good economic reports that would keep Moroccans optimistic about the future before they attempted any devaluation activities. 2017 was just such a year. It was on January 15, 2018, that the Moroccan government introduced a new "flexible exchange-rate system."[54] Morocco's leaders did not totally deregulate Morocco's currency. Rather, the Moroccan Central Bank continued to use a basket of currencies from countries with whom Morocco traded (60% from European states and 40% from the United States) to determine the price of Morocco's Dirham. But instead of letting the Dirham float only 0.3% in each direction of the established price, it expanded the band of the float to 2.5% in both directions.[55]

In 2019, it became apparent that the new program was running down the government's own reserves of foreign currency and inflating the budgets of the government's agencies which had to pay a higher price in local currency than they previously had to pay for foreign purchases. Budget increases would, of course, affect the government's credit worthiness and could, in turn, affect its bond ratings, its ability to borrow, and the interest rate at which the government could borrow. The government noted it would not further widen the band in the direction of free exchange rates as officials in the BWIs had pressed them to do.

Four other developments in Morocco's financial sector bear noting. The first is Islamic banking or participatory banking as it is called in Morocco. The second is the creation of the CFCA. The third development is a cluster of new bank initiatives to fund small- and medium-sized enterprises. And the fourth is Morocco's venture into the innovative realm of issuing Green bonds. Islamic banking will expand the number of Moroccans with bank accounts. Morocco's conventional banks kept some religious Moroccans from creating accounts because those banks charged interest which is forbidden by Sharia law. Islamic banking also brings new foreign investment into Morocco and can help to expand the economy. The CFCA is an initiative to make Moroccan financial institutions serve as a gateway for Africa, the Middle East, and Europe. Casablanca is well placed because it has a port that is a gateway to the Mediterranean Sea and to the Atlantic Ocean. The third initiative is to fund small- and medium-sized enterprises in the hopes that supporting entrepreneurship will expand employment at the local levels. The fourth initiative in Green bonds demonstrates Morocco's willingness to leapfrog into practices that are cutting edge in order to spur development. It is hoped that each of these initiatives will help Morocco's banking sector remain vital and that the first and third will help to spread the benefits of the country's banking sector to more citizens.

The introduction of Islamic banking was one of the campaign promises made by candidates of the Justice and Development Party (PJD), Morocco's religious political party, when their candidates contested parliamentary elections. Therefore, the PJD placed the introduction of such banking in Morocco on its agenda following the 2011 elections when it won the largest share of votes in parliament and its leader assumed the post of Prime Minister.

Qatar's relations with Morocco also helped pave the way for the introduction of Islamic banking and the Qatar International Islamic Bank (QIIB) became a major partner in the Umnia Bank in Morocco that became the first to offer Islamic banking. But, it took some time to establish such banks as the Moroccan government moved cautiously before the Umnia Bank was launched.

In 2010, the Moroccan government agreed to permit its existing banks to begin offering certain Islamic banking programs.[56] It was not until January

2014, however, that the PJD worked out a deal with the executive government and other parties to present a draft bill to parliament that would lay the foundation for introducing Islamic banks into Morocco. However, the Moroccan government stipulated that such banking in Morocco would be called "Participatory Finance," not Islamic Banking. Additionally, the government insisted that more time would be required for the Governor of the Bank of Al Maghrib (Morocco's Central Bank) and the Supreme Council of Ulemas (religious leaders) as well as an advisory council to sort out oversight of Islamic participatory finance institutions in Morocco.

Morocco's largest bank, Attijariwafa, which is said to be owned "by a holding company owned by Morocco's ruling monarchy" experimented with some personal finance services that are found in traditional Islamic banks.[57] Apparently, over a few years of trial, the traditional bank and its owners found no problems with moving into the realm of participatory or Islamic finances.

In 2017, the Umnia Bank opened offices in Rabat and Casablanca, and then added ten other bank branches. The QIIB is the major foreign bank that has joined in partnership to support the Umnia Bank with Morocco reserving the lion share of equity in Umnia for Moroccan-based banks. QIIB has aspirations for worldwide banking and Morocco is a logical country in which to expand since its population is over 99% Muslim. Islamic banking is practiced in over 50 countries already and Morocco's leaders studied the effects of such banking on the economy as well as the impact of such banks on the culture of countries that adopted the banks.

Morocco, which is in need of liquidity, will benefit from the external capital brought in by foreign investors like QIIB as well as from the expansion of banking accounts among its citizens. PJD government officials also have argued that the new banks will assist in keeping Morocco's conventional banks competitive. Additionally, in Morocco's related insurance sector, it was noted that with the introduction of the Takaful, or Islamic insurance, as a financial tool, it would aid the insurance sector's growth as well.[58]

In accordance with another plan to secure global resources for the Moroccan economy, the King and his administrators have set their sights on fashioning Casablanca as a regional financial hub. In 2010, they created the institution now known as the CFCA whose current name was adopted in 2014. CFCA is a public–private partnership that on an operational level is run by its own CEO and is overseen by the Casablanca Finance Commission that is Chaired by Morocco's Minister of Finance. Representatives from other government regulators in Morocco's financial sector also sit on the commission.

CFCA basically is comprised of the Central Bank (Al Maghrib), the Casablanca Stock Exchange, and La Caisse de Dépôt et de Gestion (CDG), and shares are held by various Moroccan financial sector actors.[59] From its inception, CFCA began partnering with other financial cities such as those in the United Kingdom, Germany, South Korea, etc. so that Casablanca would become noticed as a destination for investment capital.

The Casablanca Finance City (CFC) members provide the capital that flows to Morocco and then onwards to other parts of Africa, securing Morocco's place as a financial hub and increasing its reputation among other African states. In February 2018, Said Ibrahimi, Chairman of the CFCA, could state that "members of Casablanca Finance City (CFC) have so far contributed 75% of the overall investments carried out by Morocco in Africa."[60] CFC's members include such notable companies as Lloyds, Allianz, Marubeni, Mercer, and Sumitomo with 43% of the members coming from Europe, 35% from Africa, 14% from America, 5% from the Middle East, and 3% from Asia.[61] By becoming a member of CFC, foreign companies can access Morocco business advantages such as "tax incentives, a business-friendly environment, and cooperative government institutions that facilitate quick creation of legal entities and granting of licenses."[62]

CFCA also partners with its community members to offer research findings of use to many foreign investors. Its first research report was conducted by Mercer, a CFC community member and released in May 2018. It was titled, "'Human Resources Trends in Africa' and analyzed HR practices across Africa, including pay, benefits, and job mobility."[63]

While the CFCA is looking to partner with the major investment players globally and provides evidence of the modern facilities that Morocco has developed, the King and his government also recognize that it must give more attention to those who lack economic assets to compete globally. With high unemployment rates in Morocco, and employment in large industries scarce, the government's leaders, like those in many other countries, are touting entrepreneurship as a way for people, especially young educated citizens, to achieve sustainable self-employment and perhaps hire some additional workers. But as Opoku and Sandberg's research has noted, there are many barriers facing new entrepreneurs in Africa that must be addressed if the optimism surrounding such programs is to be proven correct.[64] However, Morocco, like other governments, needs to explore every opportunity for employment that it can. In March 2017, the World Bank and Morocco signed an agreement whereby the Bank provided Morocco with $50 million "for innovative startups and small and medium enterprises (SMEs)."[65] The hope was that with seed funding, after proving a business to be a good one, larger investors would step forward to scale up the SMEs. USAID has also offered to assist with trainings and outreach for entrepreneurs.

Under King Mohammed VI's leadership, Morocco has been active in securing funding from whatever sources it can. In October 2018, at an Africa Investment Summit in Berlin, the World Bank Group and the German Federal Ministry of Economic Cooperation and Development (BMZ) pledged joint action in Morocco, Tunisia, Côte d'Ivoire, Ethiopia, Ghana, and Senegal. Thus, on January 30, 2019, the World Bank Group and the German Federal Ministry of Economic Cooperation and Development (BMZ) announced that together they would provide integrated joint financial and technical support to achieve reforms that would increase private capital inflows and job creation to the six targeted countries. The sectors covered by the joint action include "renewable energy, power grid modernization, jobs and skills training, investment policy and land reform, and the development of the automotive sector."[66] It is expected that the joint effort will help spur reforms necessary to advance the sectors which, in turn, will attract new, private capital to the six countries and provide more jobs. And for Morocco's finance sector professionals, trainings to continuously upgrade their skill sets will help to make Morocco a destination for global capital.

The Moroccan government also hopes that with the creation of new small- and medium-sized businesses, it will expand its tax base. Yet, as noted earlier in this chapter, the revolt in January 2019 by the small- and medium-sized Moroccan merchants forced the government to back away from its electronic business requirements that were designed to bring in new tax revenues. The government still hopes to capture such business transactions in the future. Perhaps, it will entice new business owners to participate in electronic recordings of their business dealings through requirements for those entrepreneurs who avail themselves of the loans now being made available.

Morocco's venture into issuing Green Bonds was spurred by its ambitious efforts to develop non-carbon sources of fuel, particularly solar power. The solar Noor complex, discussed elsewhere in this volume, required an investment of about $9 billion and funds from the European Investment Bank and the World Bank helped originally to secure the project. Additionally, the Moroccan government offered guarantees to the funders and also provided energy subsidies to Moroccan consumers so they would not be adversely affected, thus demonstrating its willingness to incur government debt as part of its larger plan to gain energy sufficiency.[67]

With regard to funding, Morocco pioneered another initiative when the Moroccan Agency for Sustainable Energy (MASA) offered Green Bonds on the market to underwrite the costs of projects beyond Noor I, and the first Moroccan Green Bond was underwritten by a State guarantee.[68] Green Bonds or Climate Bonds are new financial instruments and Morocco is making good use of them and thus partially is able partially to underwrite the construction of its cutting-edge solar plant costs.

Overview of the financial sector during the first 20 years of the reign of King Mohammed VI

Two and a half years after His Majesty Mohammed VI assumed the throne, the Joint IMF–World Bank Financial Sector Assessment of Morocco reported that according to their mission's fact finding visit to Morocco in 2002, Morocco's growth was too slow, fiscal deficits were the norm, public debt was at 75% of GDP, capital accounts were restricted, the currency was pegged, and there was "limited economic linkages with the global economy and with neighboring countries."[69]

About two decades later, in 2018, it was anticipated that Morocco's economy would grow at 4.1% and its central bank had enough foreign reserves to cover five months and 24 days of imports.[70] Morocco's public debt remains high, however. In 2017, government debt was 63% of the country's GDP.[71] But as this chapter clearly demonstrates, Morocco's financial profile has greatly improved. And while the country is always seeking additional capital, it can now pick and choose the kind of capital it seeks to attract.

In July 2016, the Executive Board of the IMF approved a two-year Precautionary and Liquidity Line (PLL) arrangement of $3.61 billion for Morocco as insurance against unforeseen risks and in response to Morocco's good record of reforms. By January 2018, however, the Moroccan government had not drawn upon the IMF funding and the arrangement expired on July 21, 2018. The Moroccans did not need the precautionary funding and so chose not to take the loan. In just 20 years, Morocco's financial profile had dramatically improved.

The strategy by which Morocco has developed its financial sector over the past 20 years does not neatly adhere to any single development model. For example, despite adopting many neoliberal economic policies, Morocco has not completely unpegged its currency as it was advised to do by the BWI's officials who advocated for pristine liberal economic practices. To have done so would have been to privilege the state above its citizens to such an extreme that the resulting political unrest would, in turn, have caused the economy and the Moroccan people to suffer grievously. Over time, Morocco enacted significant exchange rate revisions but not all that the BWIs wished. Instead, King Mohammed VI seems to have focused on the growth of the financial sector in what development scholars call a "varieties of capitalism" vantage point that is closer to that of his European neighbors than to the BWI's SAP supporters. And the King and his advisors have investigated and applied every new technology and financial tool that they could employ.

Morocco also reduced its debt by 2017 through exports and through an increase in tax revenues. But the country was unable to accelerate similar progress in 2018 (and, in part, due to the global economic slump and higher oil prices, also will likely be unable to achieve such economic success again in 2019). Yet, Morocco remains an attractive country for investors still searching for an attractive investment destination.

King Mohammed VI can certainly take much of the credit for Morocco's efforts to secure capital and accelerate the country's development. In addition to the financial sector, his early efforts wisely targeted foundational sectors such as exports, energy, infrastructure, and transport. In turn, sectors like tourism and agriculture, which depend upon these foundational sectors, also have improved. Further, the King has been indefatigable in personal diplomacy with European and American corporate leaders as well as in securing business partnerships throughout Africa and parts of Asia.

The King also initiated contact with expatriates who had migrated from Morocco in order to invigorate Morocco's expatriate advisory councils in ways that deepened loyalties to Morocco and encouraged investment in the home country. The King mainly looked to the West and to Africa for his government-to-government partnerships. But he also engaged with both Russian and Chinese leaders when Morocco's interests could be furthered by looking eastward. And after careful study, the King and his advisors enacted participatory financing as a subsector of Morocco's banking sector. Morocco's King Mohammed VI has been a development entrepreneur leading his country's development trajectory.

Unfortunately, our analysis also reveals that for the average Moroccan to benefit from Morocco's financial sector investments, (1) Morocco's electronic banking needs the additional expansion of the country's digital infrastructure and (2) the interaction of Morocco's financial sector with other branches of the bureaucracy must be better managed so that, for example, local officials must not present aspiring Moroccan homeowners or business entrepreneurs with obstruction and personal requests. Morocco's financial sector has been successful in increasing housing loans for Moroccan citizens but this sector could have seen even more expansion had there been less graft when securing property and permits at the local level. Further, more affordable housing must be constructed for Moroccans. For too long, the construction companies focused on the high-end housing market for foreigners. And the state focused on high-end development projects while neglecting the needs of those with less income.

In many advanced industrial countries, when the financial sector enacts policies that expand the housing sector, it creates a major impetus for national economic development. This could also be the case in Morocco. When a consumer buys a house, it must be filled and it is domestic workers who generally produce many of the items that fill a house. Textiles, furniture, lamps, art, etc. can all be made locally and provide jobs locally. Those who construct or remodel an individual house generally are also employed locally.

In the traditional areas of a country's financial sector such as a country's debt-to-GDP ratio, exchange rate manipulation, capital account restrictions, securities markets and trading, the modernization of electronic transfers, the number of a country's banking branches, the integration of national banks into international economic structures, and the determination of interest rates, Morocco has made steady and impressive progress over the past 20 years.

However, Moroccans know that the country's financial sector is partially owned by Royals and their associates. And there is a perception that the capital in the sector is easily available to those of, or close to, the Makhzen. Further, many believe that citizens without political connections often cannot even use money when they possess it because the corruption among local government officials to process licenses and deeds is great and citizens do not possess extra currency to pay Morocco's "fees of corruption." Such perceptions produce ill will among many Moroccans and undermine their faith in the country's leadership even in a sector that has made outstanding progress.

At the end of 2018, it seems the King and his ministers were able to prevail on those in the World Bank who sympathized with the need for supporting human survival and development, as well as state financial survival, to work with Morocco to address some of the concerns that Moroccan citizens had been raising in the streets. After clearly embracing many of the neoliberal reforms of the BWIs, in 2019, World Bank officials agreed to lend assistance to Moroccan officials planning programs to address the needs of those Moroccans who were not doing well.

If Morocco is not to explode into the kind of social unrest that has plagued other Middle Eastern states in which citizens had nothing left to lose and turned their fury against state leaders, the problems of lack of employment, food, shelter, and transport must be solved. New social safety net approaches that later can be integrated into the economic fabric of the country have to be introduced.

And the financial sector has an important role to play, one that expands the country's efforts to reach Moroccans of middle and lower classes. It is up to the financial sector to support entrepreneurs, to help to expand job creation, to jump start the housing sector for Moroccans of modest means, and to find ways to lend to those who can support production linkages between rural and urban areas. Such linkages will provide some of Morocco's producers with domestic markets as a cushion against the vagaries of the international political economy and also provide citizens in rural areas with the beginnings of economic development in their life time. After 20 years, Morocco's financial sector is well placed to compete internationally. It now needs also to focus on Moroccans at home.

Notes

1 White, G. (2001). *A Comparative Political Economy of Tunisia and Morocco: On the Outside of Europe Looking In* (New York: State University of New York Press), p. 36.
2 Ezzahid, E., & Nihou, A. "Capital Deepening and Efficiency in Morocco" Munich Personal RePEc (MPRA) archive (Paper No. 82143), October 3, 2017. Posted October 24, 2017. Retrieved July 30, 2018, from https://mpra.ub.uni-muenchen.de/82143.
3 Richards, A., & Waterbury, J. (1995). *Political Economy of the Middle East: State Class and Economic Development* (Boulder, CO: Westview Press, second edition), p. 196; White, G. *A Comparative Political Economy of Tunisia and Morocco*, p. 130.
4 White, G. *A Comparative Political Economy of Tunisia and Morocco*, p. 129.
5 Cammett, M. C. (2007). *Globalization and Business Politics in Arab North Africa* (Cambridge: Cambridge University Press), pp. 84–86.
6 Ibid.
7 OPEC had promised to provide late industrializers with a cushion against its increased pricing. Unfortunately, this "cushion" was not sufficient to outweigh the costs. This was especially true for those countries who exported to advanced industrial countries (AICs) that OPEC had targeted. Those AICS' import purchases dropped as energy prices drove up the costs of goods, consumers

purchased less, and inventories mounted. The export destinations of the late industrializers dried up.

8 The Independent Evaluation Group (IEG). Retrieved August 16, 2018, from http://ieg.worldbankgroup.org/about-us.

9 World Bank Staff prepared Joint IMF-World Bank Financial Sector Assessment Program summary, Financial Sector Assessment Morocco November 2003 (based on May 2002 visit), p. 3.

10 Hassan II's brutality, imprisonment, and torture toward many political actors covered several decades and was known in Morocco as the "years of lead."

11 White, G. *A Comparative Political Economy of Tunisia and Morocco*, pp. 26–28.

12 Ibid., p. 3.

13 Ibid.

14 Ibid.

15 Ibid.

16 Such efforts were promoted internationally by the World Bank which, over time, fine-tuned its recommended budgeting techniques.

17 International Monetary Fund. (2003). Morocco: Financial System Stability Assessment IMF Country Report No. 03/212 (Washington, DC: International Monetary Fund).

18 Export.gov "Morocco Banking Systems" October 25, 2017. Accessed August 14, 2018. https://www.export.gov/article?id=Morocco-Banking-Systems

19 Oxford Group, *Morocco Report* 2018. p. 49.

20 Mühlberger, M., & Semelmann, M. (2010, May 31). "North Africa—Mediterranean Neighbors on the Rise," *Deutsche Bank Research*, p. 9.

21 U.S. Department of State Bureau of Near Eastern Affairs. (2011, April 20). *Background Note: Morocco*. http://www.state.gov/r/pa/ei/bgn/5431.htm (to BBB- from BB+ and to BBB+ from BBB, respectively).

22 Muhlberger, M., & Semelmann, M. (2010, May 31). "North Africa—Mediterranean Neighbors on the Rise," *Deutsche Bank Research*, p. 10.

23 African Markets. (2016, April 22). "About the Casablanca Stock Exchange". Retrieved January 14, 2019, from https://www.african-markets.com/en/stock-markets/bvc/about.

24 ACM-Insight. (2013, December 11). "Africa's Equity Market Capitalization" AfricaStrictlyBusiness.com. Retrieved January 25, 2019, from https://www.africastrictlybusiness.com/africas-equity-market-capitalization/. The numbers and discussion in the paragraph above are based on the reporting in this article.

25 Ibid.

26 Ibid.

27 Ibid.

28 Maghreb Arabe Presse (Rabat). (2011, August 13). *"Morocco: Nation Awarded African Country of the Future 2011/12"*. Retrieved from http://allafrica.com/stories/201108160975.html.

29 U.S. Department of State Bureau of Near Eastern Affairs, Background Note: Morocco. March 12, 2012. Retrieved from http://www.state.gov/r/pa/ei/bgn/5431.htm#econ

30 IMF Executive Board Concludes 2011 Article IV Consultation with Morocco, November 3, 2011. IMF Public Information Notice, p. 1.

31 http://www.maroc.ma/PortailInst/An/MenuGauche/Major+Projects/National+Initiative+for+Human+Development/National+Initiative+for+Human+Development.htm

32 Oxford Business Group. (2007). "Recognizable Improvement, Oxford Business Group Talks to Moulay Hafid Elalamy" in *The Report Emerging Morocco 2007* (London: Oxford Business Group, 2007), p. 52.

33 Njau, B. (2011, June 12). "Morocco Eyes Leading Offshore Service Provider Status" *Financial Times.*

34 Bazza, T. (2019, January 17). Morocco World News "Morocco's Merchants Close Shops Protesting Electronic Invoicing Law". Retrieved January 17, 2019, from https://www.moroccoworldnews.com/. The entire discussion of this episode was taken from Bazza's article in Morocco World News.

35 Morocco's Business News. (2008, October 20). "IMF Hails Morocco's Business System". Retrieved August 16, 2018, from http://www.moroccobusinessnews.com/Content/Article.asp?idr=18&id=464.

36 Ibid.

37 *apolitical*, "the Level of Banking Access". Retrieved August 17, 2018, from https://apolitical.co/solution_article/morocco-uses-postal-service-double-level-banking-access/.

38 Ibid.

39 Oxford Group, *Morocco Report 2014.* p. 61.

40 Ibid.

41 *Morocco News.* (2011, June 29). "MoneyGram International and Al Barid Bank Align to Offer Money Transfer". Retrieved August 15, 2018, from https://www.moroccoworldnews.com/2011/06/3047/moneygram-international-and-al-barid-bank-align-to-offer-money-transfer/.

42 Oxford Group, *Morocco Report 2014.* p. 61

43 Gallina, A. (2006, March). Migration, Financial Flows and Development in the Euro-Mediterranean Area. *The Journal of North African Studies*, 11(1), 19.

44 See, for example, Gallina, A. "Migration, Financial Flows and Development in the Euro-Mediterranean Area" quoting Haas, H. G. (1998). "Socio-economic Transformations and Oasis Agriculture in Southern Morocco" in L. de Haan and P. Blaikie (eds.) *Looking at Maps in the Dark: Direction for Geographical Research and Urban Environments in the Third World* (Utrech and Amsterdam: Royal Dutch Geographical Society and Faculty of Environmental Sciences, University of Amsterdam).

45 Gallina, A. "Migration, Financial Flows and Development in the Euro-Mediterranean Area" op. cit.

46 Berriane, M., & Aderghal, M. (2008). *The State of Research into International Migration from, to and through Morocco* (Country Paper: Morocco). Prepared for the African Perspectives on Human Mobility program, financed by the MacArthur Foundation.

47 *Morocco World News*, "Moroccan Diaspora Remittances Reached $6.4 Billion in 2015". Retrieved January 27, 2019, from https://www.moroccoworldnews.com/2016/04/184336/moroccan-diaspora-remittances-reached-6-4-billion-in-2015/.

48 Country Economy.com. Retrieved January 27, 2019, from https://countryeconomy.com/demography/migration/remittance/morocco.

49 Ibid.

50 Morocco's Business News, "IMF Hails Morocco's Business System", op. cit.

51 Morocco had been isolated and expelled from the Organization of African States, later the African Union, for its Western Sahara war. King Mohammed VI adeptly used FDI for good business investments, to regain standing in the eyes of other heads of state, and to help his neighbors develop so that Morocco would not have to host so many refugees en route to Europe who could not find economic activities at home.

52 Global Risk Insights. (2017, May 26). "Morocco's ambitious investments in Sub-Saharan Africa full of risks and rewards". Retrieved February 22, 2019, from https://globalriskinsights.com/2017/05/morocco-continues-to-invest-in-sub-saharan-africa/.

53 Fitch. (2017, May 11). "African Expansion Weighs on Moroccan Bank Credit Profiles". Retrieved February 22, 2019, from https://www.fitchratings.com/site/pr/1023494.
54 Lahsini,C.(2018,January21)."IMFLaudsMorocco'sNewFlexibleExchange-Rate Regime" *Morocco World News.* Retrieved July 31, 2018, from https://www.moroccoworldnews.com/2018/01/238812/imf-morocco-flexible-exchange-rate/.
55 Lahsini, C. "IMF Lauds Morocco's New Flexible Exchange-Rate Regime."
56 Morocco Tomorrow. (2012, April 1). "Morocco/Islamic banking: Morocco Eyes First Islamic Bank". Retrieved January 28, 2019, from http://www.moroccotomorrow.org/moroccoislamic-banking-morocco-eyes-first-islamic-bank/.
57 Morocco Tomorrow. (2012, April 1). "Morocco/Islamic banking: Morocco Eyes First Islamic Bank" International Islamic news Agency (IINA). Retrieved January 30, 2019, from http://www.moroccotomorrow.org/moroccoislamic-banking-morocco-eyes-first-islamic-bank/.
58 Oxford Business Group. Retrieved December 20, 2018, from https://oxfordbusinessgroup.com/search-results?sector=all&country=54044&keywords=.
59 Retrieved February 1, 2019, from http://www.casablancafinancecity.com/cfc-en/about-us/?lang=en.
60 *The North Africa Post.* February 27, 2018. Retrieved February 16, 2019, from http://northafricapost.com/22455-positive-outlook-casablanca-finance-city.html.
61 Ibid.
62 Ibid.
63 Retrieved February 1, 2019, from https://www.casablancafinancecity.com/events-en/casablanca-finance-city-initie-un-cycle-de-rapports-thematiques/?lang=en.
64 Opoku, D., & Sandberg, E. eds. (2018). *Challenges to African Entrepreneurship in the 21st Century* (New York: Palgrave MacMillan).
65 World Bank, "Morocco – Financing Innovative Startups and Small and Medium Enterprises Project". Retrieved February 1, 2019, from http://www.worldbank.org/en/news/loans-credits/2017/03/10/morocco-financing-innovative-startups-and-small-and-medium-enterprises-project.
66 World Bank. (2019, January 30). "World Bank Group and Germany Announce Enhanced Collaboration on Africa Development Projects". Retrieved February 1, 2019, from http://www.worldbank.org/en/news/press-release/2019/01/30/world-bank-group-and-germany-announce-enhanced-collaboration-on-africa-development-projects.
67 Op. cit. Domonoske, C. "Morocco Unveils A Massive Solar Power Plant In The Sahara".
68 MASEN. (2016, April 11). "African Climate Finance Pioneer Issues Morocco's First Ever Green Bond." Press Release. Retrieved March 9, 2019, from http://www.masen.ma/en/actualites/.
69 World Bank Staff, Financial Sector Assessment (FSA) Morocco November 2003.
70 Yaakoubi, A. E. (2018, January 14). "Morocco Looks for Smooth Transition to More Flexible Exchange-Rate System". *Reuters.* Retrieved August 17, 2018, from https://www.reuters.com/article/morocco-currency/morocco-looks-for-smooth-transition-to-more-flexible-exchange-rate-system-idUSL8N1P90D0.
71 *Trading Economics.* "Morocco Government Debt to GDP". Retrieved February 16, 2019, from https://tradingeconomics.com/morocco/government-debt-to-gdp.

3 Liberalizing the telecommunications sector

The liberalization of Morocco's telecommunications sector has been seen as a success worthy of international investment.[1] Beginning with the decision to privatize, government policy has helped the sector grow from an anemic single supplier to one of the best in the region. Rather than rely on a laissez faire model, King Mohammed VI selectively supported programs, which has resulted in greater access and technology. Over the past two decades, the sector's development has been an important achievement in its own right, and its full impact has reverberated throughout society and allowed the country's economy to better compete in the globalized marketplace. The proliferation of digital technology has connected the world like never before and the King's innovative steps to embrace this change ensured it kept pace with other countries.

In the middle of the 1990s, King Hassan II decided that he wanted the country to become a regional leader in telecommunications and began opening the sector through to privatization and competition. Mohammed VI continued the liberalization policies of his father, but accompanied them with evolving five-year strategic plans that helped support a significant expansion in access throughout Morocco. These government interjections, like a unique reinvestment plan known as "pay or play," increased the sector's technological capabilities and helped lead an expansion into West and Central Africa. The achievements of the industry are impressive. There are now more cell phone contracts than Moroccans; internet and computers are increasingly seen as staples rather than luxury goods; and the majority of cell phone users have smartphones. Nevertheless, the opportunity for growth within the sector remains, particularly in e-commerce and other digital enterprises.

The government took its first steps toward modernization in 1997 by enacting Law 24–96, which initiated the sector's reform from a single operator into a competitive industry. Before 1997, the state-run National Post Office and Telecommunications Agency (ONPT) operated both the national postal service and the country's telephone service. But the ONPT suffered from budget deficits and poor service quality. When the internet was first introduced in Morocco in 1995, it became increasingly clear that the ONPT was not sustainable, especially if the country's economy was going to continue to develop and grow.[2]

First, Law 24–96 separated the post office from telecommunications. Originally known as *Ittisalat Al Maghrib*, the law created Maroc Telecom and opened the new company up to private investment. At the same time, the law created the National Telecommunications Regulatory Agency (ANRT) to oversee the industry and lead the government's selective development policies. Not only did King Hassan II want to be a regional leader, he recognized the importance of effective telecommunications for economic development and adopted the administrative framework necessary to support the sector's growth.[3]

In support of this effort, Morocco's Ministry of Industry and Trade created a body to investigate the steps the government might take to improve the sector. The Secrétariat d'Etat aux Postes et Technologies de l'Information (SEPTI) was responsible for developing information and communication technology (ICT) strategies for the government and helped develop plans focused on supporting protection of commercial and personal information, digital literacy, financing new enterprises, and access.[4] However, as Anastassios Gentzoglanis, Nancy Sundberg, and Susan Schorr note in their early study of the industry's development, SEPTI's roles overlapped with ANRT causing confusion and consternation.[5]

Morocco's initial reforms in the telecommunications sector supported its overall strategy to liberalize the economy in order to attract new investments. When King Mohammed VI ascended the throne in 1999, he supported and expanded the initiative. By 2000, the strategy seemed to pay off when the French telecommunications group Vivendi paid $2.4 billion for a 35% stake in Maroc Telecom.[6] Vivendi purchased additional stock from the government for $1.2 billion, increasing its shares to 51% and majority ownership in 2004.[7] The French company then sold their shares to Etisalat, a multinational Emirati-based telecommunications company partially owned by the United Arab Emirates government, in 2014 for $5.7 billion.[8] The Moroccan government still holds 30% of the shares and maintains influence over the company's supervisory board and board chairman,[9] although it announced in June 2019 that it plans to sell 8% of its shares.[10] Nevertheless, Etisalat has helped Maroc Telecom expand its services outside of Morocco as well as improve its service inside the country.[11]

In 1999, the Kingdom offered its second telecommunications license to Orange Maroc, originally known as Meditel. The company originally purchased its license for $1.1 billion and began to challenge Maroc Telecom's monopoly over market share.[12] Both the original Vivendi purchase and Meditel's purchase were analyzed to be the most profitable telecommunications transactions for any emerging market at that time.[13] Ownership of Orange Maroc is currently divided between the French-based multinational telecommunications company Orange, FinanceCom (owned by Othman Benjelloun, Morocco's wealthiest private citizen), and the CDG Group (a state-run pension fund).[14]

Then, in 2005, Morocco offered its third license to INWI (previously known as Wana), which is controlled by the royal family's private holding company,

Société Nationale d'Investissement or National Investment Company (SNI). The Kuwaiti telecom company Zain, whose largest shareholder is Kuwait's sovereign wealth fund, is the other primary investor with a 15.5% stake.[15]

While the three main companies are privately controlled, a success from the original liberalization efforts, the King has retained influence over the industry. The government maintains shares in two of the three firms, granting it influence in management, while the King's holding company owns the majority of shares in the third. In addition, the King controls the power of appointment over the regulatory agency. The director of the ANRT is appointed (and dismissed) by the King and the board is chaired by the prime minister and includes the ANRT director and several government ministers.[16] This neither guarantees effectiveness nor prohibits development, but it has allowed the King to maintain his political reach throughout the country.

Meanwhile, the evolution of the industry and its impact on society and the economy cannot be understated. According to Hsain Ilahiane, maybe the most successful aspect of the early liberalization efforts, "beyond simply awakening to the prospects of ICTs as an engine of economic growth," is the creation of what is known in Morocco as, "the new culture of the market."[17] Or as one Moroccan telecommunications official told Ilahiane,

> By catering to the diverse needs of consumers, the new Telecom operators have been successful in fostering not only a culture of 'consumer is king', but also managed to smooth the transition to getting consumers used to the idea of new technological features and types of mobile technologies.[18]

By 2005, the country had ten million mobile phone subscribers, approximately one-third of the population and a 300% increase compared to 2000, when only 10% of the population held mobile subscriptions.[19] The government's next step was the implementation of local-loop unbundling, announced in 2006 through the Prime Minister's Order 3-3-06, which allowed the three carriers to share infrastructure.[20] This was an important step to be able to provide service to all customers and allow for equal competition rather than limiting the carrier options based on location.

Morocco's telecommunications improvements also had an impact on small businesses. As Ilahiane found, the advancements over the past couple decades improved the lives of individual Moroccans, including lower-income entrepreneurs who employed mobile phones to both "intensify and extend local and non-local forms of communications…to create new pockets of entrepreneurship."[21] The study showed that the interviewees, although they did not own a computer or have access to the internet, were able to use their mobile phones to increase their income by 56%.[22]

In 2004, ready to move beyond the initial focus on privatization and performance, King Mohammed VI released a plan called *e-Morocco* that sought to expand access across the country and position Morocco as a leader in ICT.[23] Law 55-01 was introduced to help implement e-Morocco and open the market further to entice additional private and international investment.[24] Trying to improve access, the law required operators to allocate 2% of revenues for infrastructure development, particularly for remote and rural areas throughout the country.[25] The rule became known as "pay or play" because companies could either create their own projects, valued at 2% of revenues, or contribute to the newly created Universal Service Fund (USF) directly. Widely viewed as a success, the fund has incentivized telecommunications infrastructure development that has been critical in continuing to improve the country's performance, capabilities, and access.

By 2010, the country was offering 3G high-speed mobile broadband service for the first time and had surpassed 30 million mobile phone subscribers, an additional 20 million subscriptions – more than three-fifths of the population – in just five years.[26] By 2015, the number of subscribers surpassed the population (33 million) and 4G, the best data and voice technology of the time, was available for mobile phone subscribers.[27] The majority of Moroccan phone subscriptions skipped landline services and went directly to mobile services (92.7%); and overwhelmingly subscribers used pre-pay services (38.5 million) compared to contract services (2.9 million).[28] In addition, the industry was accounting for 7%[29] of Morocco's GDP and expecting to see 5% annual growth through 2020, according to the London-based consultancy Pyramid Research.[30]

By 2018, the three major firms controlled the overwhelming majority of the market and found their niche to maintain their competitiveness and market share. The old state-run company, Maroc Telecom, holds the largest market share in internet (53.3%), mobile (44.2%), and fixed-line phone service (92.1%), which can be credited to legacy customers and Etisalat's investment.[31] Orange Maroc controls almost one-quarter of the internet market share and nearly one-third of the mobile customers.[32] It was also the first operator to launch 4G in Morocco and boasts over 5,000 kilometers of fiber optic cable.[33] INWI, meanwhile, controls approximately one-quarter of internet and mobile business in Morocco and 30% of the market's fixed wireless internet, which can be particularly beneficial in rural areas where normal wireless coverage can be inconsistent.[34]

Over the past 20 years, the King has transformed the sector from a state-run, poor-performing single firm to a multi-firm industry that has improved service to include the newest and most advanced technology and expanded access to the entire population. Samantha Muwafaq Constant, writing for the World Bank, credits Morocco's success to three factors: (1) prioritization of technology improvements; (2) a youthful, educated, and eager population; and (3) expanding private competition that emphasized technical requirements, innovation, quality, and access.[35] In addition, the European Bank for Reconstruction and Development lauded Morocco for its legal and regulatory regime, particularly the sector's organization and governance like its innovative "pay or play" reinvestment scheme.[36]

One USF-funded project allocated one billion dirhams to provide multimedia equipment to 9,000 schools, whereas another sent computers to over 150,000 teachers across the country.[37] The PACTE program (2008–2011), another USF project, expanded mobile coverage to nearly every populated area in Morocco, including some of the most remote areas of Morocco.[38] The program cost approximately 1.44 billion dirhams and helped reach 2 million rural Moroccans.[39] The USF also provided 120 million dirhams worth of digital equipment to universities and training centers in 2011, and spent 246 million dirhams on computers with mobile broadband from 2009 to 2013, improving the education for 80,000 students.[40]

Another one of Mohammed VI's goals for the sector, as King Hassan II had originally identified, was to develop the industry to compete regionally. Leading this effort has been Maroc Telecom. Spurred by Etisalat's leadership, the company expanded its business in West and Central Africa, and as of 2017, 65% of Maroc Telecom's 35 million customers and over 43% of its revenue came from outside Morocco, according to the company's financial report.[41] Maroc Telecom first entered foreign markets in 2001 when it partnered with Mauritel in Mauritania and expanded its regional reach in 2014 when it acquired Etisalat's subsidiaries in Benin, Ivory Coast, Gabon, Niger, Togo, and the Central African Republic.[42]

Morocco has also come out in support of the 2018 Group of 5 (G5) Sahel Priority Investment Program, which among other projects, is looking to enhance the G5 countries' telecommunications infrastructure.[43] Having already expanded its domestic network to rural areas like the five countries are attempting to do, Morocco is well equipped to provide support. In addition, this provides Moroccan firms, particularly Maroc Telecom, opportunities for further expansion and investment into new markets. Morocco has also made a renewed effort to join the Economic Community of West African States (ECOWAS), which could help further integrate the telecommunications sector into West Africa.[44]

The King's efforts to internationalize the sector has also meant pursuing opportunities that can provide domestic jobs. The Casablanca Technopark has attracted offshore services like call centers, which has led to jobs and investment. In fact, call centers have taken advantage of the country's French language skills to become a significant employment opportunity (approximately 30,000 in 2012).[45]

But the development of the internet has had the greatest impact on society and provides the largest potential for economic development. According to the ANRT's 2017 survey, more than 70% of households had access to the internet, a 181% increase from 2010 and an annual average growth rate of 16%.[46] In addition, nearly 60% of all Moroccans own a computer or tablet, a 72% increase from 2010, and nearly half of computer owners have more than one device.[47] These figures demonstrate that the internet and computers have become staples for the majority of Moroccans, no longer cost prohibitive or viewed as luxury goods.

Government efforts to improve access have eliminated vast dead zones, but rural areas continue to lag behind urban centers in computer ownership, according to the survey. Only one-third of rural households own a computer; however, ownership has been increasing by 27% per year and the majority of rural households own a mobile phone.[48] At the same time, there has also been a proliferation of smartphones as nearly three-quarters of all mobile phone subscribers are using smartphones, giving them access to the internet anywhere in the country.[49]

Unlike other countries in the region, Bouziane Zaid notes that the government control over the internet has remained limited, albeit uneven, allowing Moroccans to create and publish relatively freely on the internet.[50] And most users have flocked to social media to consume and produce content. In 2011, 67% of Moroccans who accessed the internet did so to use social media; by 2017, more than 90% were using social media.[51] In 2011, Morocco was the third highest user of Facebook in the region, the most popular social media platform globally. Between 2015 and 2017, the number of Facebook users more than tripled, and Morocco still remains one of the top countries in the Arab region with nearly 15 million users.[52] Among the myriad of social media applications available, in 2017 Moroccans were using the messaging app WhatsApp (92.4%) most frequently, then Facebook (82.7%) and YouTube (49.5%).[53] Importantly, as Mohamed el Marzouki has shown, social media is creating a more politically active and engaged Moroccan,[54] where over 80% use the internet to access and follow the news.[55]

However, less than half of all Moroccans were using the internet for work and only 20% for school or research in 2017.[56] This is not only a lost opportunity, but in a globalized world, Morocco will need to improve in these areas if it wants to compete against other emerging countries. And the King understands the necessity to expand the use of the internet. Not satisfied with its initial success by 2013, the King announced a new government initiative, Maroc Numeric (Digital Morocco) that emphasized e-government capabilities, computerization among small- and medium-sized enterprises (SMEs), and support for domestic businesses exporting information technologies services.[57] Notably, the infrastructure and technological advancements have allowed the country to turn its attention, as evidenced by Maroc Numeric, to the benefits the industry could achieve across numerous sectors of the economy. Although, some foreign companies' investment, dependent on technological communications, have found that it is not just high-technology attainment in Morocco that will ensure the success of their businesses.

For example, the decision by Uber to stop operating in Morocco is instructive.[58] In addition to the loss for consumers and their integration of mobile applications into daily use, it hinders the country's ability to learn from one of the leading tech companies and apply its skills and techniques in a local business environment. And the learning curve among Moroccans is still steep. Only one-third know how to send an email with an attachment and less than one-quarter shop for goods and services or use online banking.[59] The largest hurdle to more e-commerce is the lack of trust (75.4%) among internet users, according to ANRT.[60] But at the same time, since the majority of Moroccans now use the internet, there is a significant opportunity for growth within the local tech sector, albeit with a learning curve.

The King's efforts to improve the telecommunications industry are commendable. The country's progress over the past two decades to increase competition and privatization have resulted in enhanced capabilities, accessibility, and usage; nevertheless, challenges remain. Like all industries reliant on technology, continued improvements within the sector are still needed for Morocco to reach its goals. As Constant correctly identifies, the Kingdom needs to continue to address affordability, enhance digital literacy particularly among older and rural populations, and cultivate the next generation of e-content and software producers and developers.[61] As of 2011, only 6% of those on the internet used online banking or e-commerce activities.[62] Eight years later, that had only doubled to 12%.[63] Internet usage is currently driven by the youth (ages 15–29) who use the internet and applications on their phones, in part, to find ways that positively impact their livelihoods. And Morocco can harness that potential for further growth in areas the youth care about and in a sector that is a relatively lower threshold of entry compared to banking, aeronautics, or mining.

However, despite its relative independence compared to other Arab countries, the state's influence on the sector remains a concern. The government owns minority stakes in Maroc Telecom and Orange Maroc, while the King privately owns the majority stake in the third largest telecom company. In addition, the King not only maintains appointment power over the regulatory agency, the government sits on the board. This diminishes the ANRT's independence and creates a conflict of interest where business owners conduct their own oversight. The possibility for financial corruption and the government's ability to co-opt the industry, particularly on issues deemed to be a national security threat, are of most concern. The government has cracked down on political activists using surveillance tools, controlled online content, and in rare cases even shut down service.[64] But it also operates in more subtle ways, incentivizing control. For example, Bouziane Zaid notes how the three telecommunication companies have been known to withdraw advertising money from news outlets that challenge the state's news narrative, pressuring media to stay on message or risk insolvency.[65]

Social media may be creating a more engaged Moroccan, but this concern has led the government to use vaguely defined terms within legislation like the 2003 anti-terrorism law to restrict free speech through intimidation and arrests.[66] Additionally, ANRT restricted Voice over Internet Protocol (VoIP) services like Skype, Facebook, and WhatsApp claiming they violated Article 1 of the telecommunications law due to the lack of a proper service license.[67] Saad Guerraoui noted that the decision was likely a response from the main three operators complaining about a major drop in call volumes, particularly international calls.[68] The Brookings Institution calculated that the ban likely cost Morocco $320 million in economic losses.[69] Nearly one year later and just days before the UN Climate Change Conference COP 22 was held in Marrakech, the ban was quietly lifted.[70] This action appeared to be a clear attempt to avoid international condemnation.

The government has also been known to use phishing spyware (as early as 2012), for example when it infiltrated the news site Mamfakinch which became popular over its coverage of the February 20th Movement.[71] The government created the High Authority for Audiovisual Communication (HACA) in 2002 and the National Control Commission for the Protection of Personal Data (CNDP) in 2007, which in addition to the ANRT, are supposed to regulate and protect consumers.[72] However, as Samia Errazzouki argues, these agencies create the "illusion of institutional independence," but in fact have given the government "greater leverage over the field."[73] The government's use of surveillance tools follows a pattern around the world that has seen new technologies democratize access to information, but with both positive and negative consequences.[74] At the same time, Morocco's actions to control political activism, or protect the operators' profit margins, risk thwarting innovation and risk-taking by entrepreneurs and SMEs who fear government overreach may threaten their business model or economic livelihood.

Nevertheless, it is clear that the enhancements to the telecommunications sector have allowed the country to compete across numerous sectors and spurred economic growth. As we will see in later chapters, the expansion and modernization of the telecommunications sector was critical in creating the business ecosystem multinational corporations like Renault needed to invest in a major plant in Morocco. And, as discussed in Chapter 5, such investment proved to international financial institutions that their support for the world's largest solar power plant in Morocco would be a worthwhile investment. And the King has refused to rest on his laurels. With the institutions in place, the government continues to work with firms to update laws and improve infrastructure. For example, in February 2018, the ANRT issued an amendment to Law 121-12 to improve consumer protections, enhance broadband, and strengthen regulatory levers.[75]

What is clear is that in a remarkably short amount of time, Morocco's King Mohammed VI understood the importance modern telecommunications was going to play in the global economy and that Morocco needed to dramatically improve its infrastructure and capabilities in order to implement its national development strategies. Yet, there are still potential areas of expansion. While Nokia, Samsung, and other multinational telecommunications corporations have opened for business in Morocco, a vast digital marketplace remains underutilized. Young Moroccans have an opportunity to build on the success of the last two decades and develop more digital businesses. In 2010, there was optimism that communication, computer, and information services were surging as exports had increased 13% from a decade earlier, but with the continued lag in Moroccans purchasing goods and services online, the progress has not kept pace with the opportunities and infiltrated the domestic market.[76]

The King has taken steps to address some of the concerns slowing the expanded use of the internet. For example, the government has improved its transportation infrastructure allowing for more timely deliveries and improved internet business regulation, both significant concerns among internet users and online shoppers.[77] Among the myriad of challenges facing the country, King Mohammed VI continues to be forward looking within the telecommunications sector, providing the opportunity for continued development. In order to further economic growth in the internet age, he will need to continue to do so.

Notes

1 Sutherland, E. (2015). Bribery and Corruption in Telecommunications – the Kingdom of Morocco. *Info*, 17(2), 16–35. doi:10.1108/info-11-2014-0048 (p. 16).
2 Constant, S. M. (2011). *Broadband in Morocco: Political Will Meets Socioeconomic Reality*. Washington, DC: infoDev/World Bank. Retrieved from http://www.broadband-toolkit.org/ (p. 2).
3 Ilahiane, H. (2011). Mobile Phone Use, Bricolage, and the Transformation of Social and Economic Ties of Micro-Entrepreneurs in Urban Morocco. *International Journal of Business Anthropology*, 2(1), 31–49. Retrieved from http://search.ebscohost.com.proxy1.library.jhu.edu/login.aspx?direct=true&db=bsu&AN=60782918&site=ehost-live&scope=site (p. 34).
4 Gentzoglanis, A., Sundberg, N., & Schorr, S. (2001). *Effective Regulation – Case Study: Morocco* (Rep.). International Telecommunications Union. Retrieved from https://www.itu.int/ITU-D/treg/Case_Studies/effective-regulation/Maroc.pdf (pp. 8–9).
5 Ibid., p. 41.
6 Ilahiane, H. (2013). Catenating the Local and the Global in Morocco: How Mobile Phone Users Have Become Producers and Not Consumers. *The Journal of North African Studies*, 18(5), 652–667. doi:10.1080/13629387.2013.849894 (p. 655).
7 Sutherland, E. (2015) "Bribery and corruption in telecommunications – the Kingdom of Morocco", p. 23.
8 Ibid.
9 *2016 Registration Document: Including the Annual Financial Report* (Rep.). (2017, April 14). Retrieved from https://www.iam.ma/Lists/TelechargementFinance/Attachments/997/2016 Registration Document_en.pdf (p. 33).
10 Lystad, J. (2019, June 3) Moroccan Government to Sell Shares in Maroc Telecom. *Morocco World News*. Retrieved from https://www.moroccoworldnews.com/2019/06/274921/morocco-sells-maroc-telecom-shares/.
11 Ibid., pp. 6–8.
12 Ilahiane, H. (2013). Catenating the Local and the Global in Morocco: How Mobile Phone Users Have Become Producers and Not Consumers. p. 655.
13 Ibid.
14 Orange. (n.d.). *Actionnariat*. Retrieved November 13, 2018, from http://corporate.orange.ma/A-propos-d-Orange-au-Maroc/Actionnariat.
15 Zain. (n.d.). *Overview*. Retrieved November 13, 2018, from https://www.zain.com/en/about-us/overview/.

16 Sutherland, E. (2015). "Bribery and Corruption in Telecommunications – the Kingdom of Morocco", p. 18.
17 Ilahiane, H. (2011). *Mobile Phone Use, Bricolage, and the Transformation of Social and Economic Ties of Micro-Entrepreneurs in Urban Morocco*, p. 35.
18 Ibid.
19 Sarrocco, C. (2004, February 25). *Shaping the Future Mobile Information Society: The Case of Morocco* (Working paper). Retrieved from https://www.itu.int/osg/spu/ni/futuremobile/general/casestudies/Moroccocase.pdf (p. 16).
20 Sutherland, E. (2015). "Bribery and Corruption in Telecommunications – the Kingdom of Morocco", p. 19.
21 Ilahiane, H. (2013). *Catenating the Local and the Global in Morocco: How Mobile Phone Users Have Become Producers and Not Consumers*, p. 654.
22 Ibid., p. 657.
23 Constant, S. W. (2011). *Broadband in Morocco: Political Will Meets Socio-economic Reality*, p. 2.
24 Ibid., p. 5.
25 Ibid., p. 17.
26 Telecom Sector in Brief. (n.d.). Retrieved December 5, 2018, from https://www.anrt.ma/en/indicateurs/secteur-des-telecoms-en-bref.
27 *Rapport Annuel 2014* (Rep.). (n.d.). Retrieved from https://www.anrt.ma/sites/default/files/Ra_Annuel_ Anrt2014.pdf (p. 10).
28 Ibid., p. 22.
29 Morocco – Telecommunications. (n.d.). Retrieved from https://www.export.gov/article?id=Morocco-Telecommunications-Prospect.
30 New Investments and Expanding Penetration Support Growth in Morocco's Telecoms Sector. (2017, January 24). Retrieved January 4, 2019, from https://oxfordbusinessgroup.com/overview/moving-new-investments-and-expanding-penetration-support-growth-0.
31 *2016 Registration Document: Including the Annual Financial Report*, p. 5.
32 *Welcome to Orange Morocco*. (2017, May 4). Retrieved December 17, 2018, from https://www.orange.com/en/Group/Orange-in-the-world/countries/Welcome-to-Orange-Marocco.
33 Orange. (n.d.). *Orange au Maroc en chiffres*. Retrieved November 13, 2018, from https://corporate.orange.ma/A-propos-d-Orange-au-Maroc/Orange-au-Maroc-en-chiffres.
34 Inwi en chiffres. (n.d.). Retrieved 2018, from https://www.inwi.ma/corporate/inwi-en-chiffres.
35 Constant, S. M. (2011). *Broadband in Morocco: Political Will Meets Socio-economic Reality*, p. viii.
36 *2012 Electronic Communication Sector Comparative Assessment: Morocco – Country Summary* (Rep.). (2012, November 15). Retrieved from https://www.ebrd.com/downloads/legal/telecomms/morocco-2012.pdf (p. 22).
37 Ibid., p. 35.
38 National Telecommunications Regulatory Agency. (n.d.). *PACTE*. Retrieved March 1, 2019, from https://www.anrt.ma/en/missions/service-universel/pacte.
39 Ibid.
40 Constant, S. M. (2011), p. 17.
41 *Financial Report 2017* (Rep.). (n.d.). Retrieved from https://www.iam.ma/Lists/TelechargementFinance/Attachments/1043/Financial report 2017_en.pdf (p. 20).
42 Ibid., pp. 7–8.
43 *Priority Investment Program (PIP/G5 Sahel) First Phase 2019–2021* (Rep.). (2018, October). Retrieved from https://www.g5sahel.org/images/DOCPIP/PIP_G5S_EN__VF.pdf.

44 Fabiani, R. (2018, March 28). Morocco's Difficult Path to ECOWAS Membership. Retrieved from https://carnegieendowment.org/sada/75926.
45 Elaalaoui, A. (2012, January 17). The Growing Call Center Industry in Morocco. *Morocco World News.* Retrieved from https://www.moroccoworldnews.com/2012/01/23053/the-growing-call-center-industry-in-morocco/.
46 *ICTs Usage in Households and by Individuals 2017 Results Synthesis* (Rep.). (2018, October 24). Retrieved from https://www.anrt.ma/sites/default/files/publications/results-ict_survey_2017_eng-edited_24102018_0.pdf (p. 8).
47 Ibid., p. 8.
48 Ibid., p. 20.
49 Ibid., p. 8.
50 Zaid, B. (2017). The Authoritarian Trap in State/Media Structures in Morocco's Political Transition. *The Journal of North African Studies*, 22(3), 340–360. doi:10.1080/13629387.2017.1307910.
51 *ICTs Usage in Households and by Individuals 2017 Results Synthesis*, p. 52.
52 Salem, F. (2017). *The Arab Social Media Report 2017: Social Media and the Internet of Things: Towards Data-Driven Policymaking in the Arab World* (Rep. No. 7). Retrieved from http://www.mbrsg.ae/getattachment/1383b88a-6eb9-476a-bae4-61903688099b/Arab-Social-Media-Report-2017 (p. 37).
53 *ICTs Usage in Households and by Individuals 2017 Results Synthesis.* (2018, October 24). p. 62.
54 Marzouki, M. E. (2018). Citizens of the Margin: Citizenship and Youth Participation on the Moroccan Social Web. *Information, Communication & Society*, 21(1), 147–161. doi:10.1080/1369118X.2016.1266373.
55 Ibid. *ICTs Usage in Households and by Individuals 2017 Results Synthesis*, p. 28.
56 Ibid.
57 Constant, S. M. (2011). *Broadband in Morocco: Political Will Meets Socio-economic Reality*, pp. 6–7.
58 Fioretti, J. (2018, February 19). Uber Suspends Service in Morocco After Two Years. *Reuters.* Retrieved from https://uk.reuters.com/article/us-uber-morocco/uber-suspends-service-in-morocco-after-two-years-idUKKCN1G31Z0.
59 *ICTs Usage in Households and by Individuals 2017 Results Synthesis.* (2018, October 24). p. 44.
60 Ibid., p. 66.
61 Constant, S. M. (2011). *Broadband in Morocco: Political Will Meets Socio-economic Reality*, p. viii.
62 Ibid., p. 18.
63 *ICTs Usage in Households and by Individuals 2017 Results Synthesis.* (2018, October 24). p. 52.
64 Nieves, E. (2017, July 27). Fighting for Basic Rights in Morocco. *New York Times.* Retrieved from https://lens.blogs.nytimes.com/2017/07/27/fighting-for-basic-rights-in-morocco/.
65 Zaid, B. (2017). The Authoritarian Trap in State/Media Structures in Morocco's Political Transition, p. 346.
66 *Freedom on the Net 2017: Morocco Country Report.* (2018, October 11). Retrieved from https://freedomhouse.org/report/freedom-net/2017/morocco.
67 West, D. M. (2016, October 6). Global Economy Loses Billions from Internet Shutdowns [Web blog post]. Retrieved from https://www.brookings.edu/blog/techtank/2016/10/06/global-economy-loses-billions-from-internet-shutdowns/.
68 Guerraoui, S. (2016, March 9). Morocco Banned Skype, Viber, WhatsApp and Facebook Messenger. It Didn't Go Down Well. *Middle East Eye.* Retrieved from https://www.middleeasteye.net/opinion/morocco-banned-skype-viber-whatsapp-and-facebook-messenger-it-didnt-go-down-well.
69 West, D. M. (2016, October 6).

70 Kessio, B. (2016, October 24). Morocco's VoIP Ban Quietly Reversed without Official Announcement. *Morocco World News*. Retrieved from https://www.moroccoworldnews.com/2016/10/199712/moroccos-voip-ban-quietly-reversed-without-official-announcement/.
71 Errazzouki, S. (2017). Under Watchful Eyes: Internet Surveillance and Citizen Media in Morocco, the Case of Mamfakinch. *The Journal of North African Studies*, 22(3), 361–385. doi:10.1080/13629387.2017.1307907 (p. 373).
72 Ibid., p. 375.
73 Ibid.
74 Zaid, B. (2016). Internet and Democracy in Morocco: A Force for Change and an Instrument for Repression. *Global Media and Communication*, 12(1), 49–66. doi:10.1177/1742766515626826 (pp. 50–51).
75 Promulgation of the Law No. 121-12, Relating to the Post and Telecommunications. (2019, February 18). Retrieved from https://www.anrt.ma/en/lagence/actualites/promulgation-law-no-121-12-relating-post-and-telecommunications.
76 Achy, L. (2013, November). *Structural Transformation and Industrial Policy in Morocco* (Working paper No. 796). Retrieved from https://ideas.repec.org/p/erg/wpaper/796.html (p. 9).
77 *ICTs Usage in Households and by Individuals 2017 Results Synthesis*. (2018, October 24). pp. 66–67.

4 Transportation, industrial production, and trade

Taking advantage of its niche geographical position in a globalized world

As a part of its larger economic development strategy, Morocco has taken advantage of its niche geographical position to situate the country as a major transportation hub in the global marketplace. By enhancing the ports, privatizing the auto industry, and upgrading the infrastructure, the Kingdom has attracted strategic investments from multinational corporations (MNCs) that have increased exports and supported domestic growth in numerous sectors of the economy. Similar to Morocco's energy strategy (analyzed in Chapter 5), which has also taken advantage of its geographical location, the transportation sector has seen international firms move production to Morocco for lower labor costs and quick access to European Union (EU) markets, as well as for trade to and from Africa and the Americas.

Rather than liberalizing the economy in the laissez-faire model, the King identified specific sectors where he believed Morocco had regional and international advantages. The country used its strategic location but also sought to attract original equipment manufacturers (OEMs), like Renault, through preferential investment incentives that would then entice suppliers down the supply chain to follow the OEM. The King then focused on supporting and expanding local small- and medium-sized enterprises (SMEs) to build the country's domestic industrial base.

As a result, between 1999 and 2013, productivity increased by 3.7%; nearly 13% of the improvement came from labor reallocation toward sectors with above average productivity, like the aeronautics and automotive industries, whereas the rest came from technological upgrades and capital accumulation.[1] Mohammed Rachid, deputy director for international relations and organizations at Casablanca Finance City, told the Oxford Business Group, "What the performance of the automotive industry has shown, and to a smaller extent the performance of aeronautics, is that industrialisation [sic] can in fact work in Morocco."[2]

The Kingdom's earlier success in the 2000s led the country to release its latest industrial policy initiative in 2014. The Plan for Industrial Acceleration (PAI) builds on previous efforts to turn around and support numerous sectors that the King identified as areas of potential growth. The PAI markets the country as "a well connected [sic] country where the movement of people, goods and data is smooth and rapid."[3]

The PAI's goals are ambitious, including increasing the percent of GDP generated from industry from 14% to 23%, creating 500,000 new jobs by 2020, reducing the balance of trade, and improving SME's integration into the global value chain.[4] To achieve these goals, the initiative identified numerous areas of government intervention that could support private growth such as the creation of industrial ecosystems, which would foster partnerships between business leaders and SMEs, and increase the technology transferred and local value added.[5] In addition, the PAI initiated specific targeted measures including providing various industry trainings, tax credits, technology support measures, and the creation of the Industrial Development Fund.[6] And finally, the initiative has tried to take advantage of Morocco's international position by working with other African countries, attracting more foreign direct investment (FDI), and utilizing its existing free trade agreements.[7] According to the World Bank, the PAI is attempting to address three main weaknesses in Morocco's economy: access to financing for industrial projects, access to land and integrated platforms, and quality training for the appropriate sector.[8]

In order to attract OEMs and other global suppliers to invest, Morocco needed to improve its transportation infrastructure: its ports, roads, and railways. Since 2000, the King has dedicated approximately 300 billion dirhams to constructing, expanding, and connecting ports to the globalized trading network through the National Port Strategy 2030, adding tens of thousands of kilometers of roads within and between cities through Plan Route 2035, and expanding the rail network for passenger and cargo trains throughout the country in Plan Rail 2035, including the continent's first high-speed rail line that became operational at the end of 2018.[9] The PAI has also been supported by the National Logistics Strategy 2030, which should help interconnect the various sectors, reduce costs, and increase the ease of doing business.

Marco Rensma and Saad Hamoumi's research offers an insightful profile of business opportunities in Morooco and of the country's efforts to bolster its transportation sector. According to Rensma and Hamoumi, the King expects to spend an additional 400 billion dirhams by 2035 in order to complete the country's transportation infrastructure projects, and hopes to involve the private sector more through public-private partnerships.[10] Since 2010, public investments in the transportation sector have surpassed 15 billion dirhams per year and reached as high as 31 billion dirhams in 2017; on average, the funds were divided between rail (5.7 billion dirhams), maritime (5 billion dirhams), and road (7.8 billion dirhams) projects.[11] Morocco's transport and logistics sector employs about one million Moroccans and contributes about 4% to GDP.[12] But the sector's most valuable contribution is its attractiveness to investors in other sectors who will take advantage of the improvements that are being made in the transportation sector to make their businesses more efficient.

Transportation infrastructure

Ports are a crucial part of the King's development plans. Not only does the overwhelming majority of the country's foreign trade come and go by sea, but in order to entice MNCs to invest in factories and plants, they need to have confidence in the capabilities and timeliness of the ports. Morocco's vast coastline has allowed the country to develop 35 sea ports, 11 of which are designed for international trade, 18 for the fishing industry, and six marinas.[13] In 2010, the ports could intake a maximum of 70 million tons of cargo (excluding transshipments that use Moroccan ports to transfer ships on its way to its final destination).[14] By 2016, that number had almost reached 90 million tons, a 29% increase in just six years.[15] The Ministry of Equipment and Transport intends to increase that total port capacity to 140 million tons by 2030, and with transshipments included, to surpass 300 million tons.[16]

Increasingly, the Tanger Med port, which cost more than $1 billion to construct, is becoming the most important in Morocco and in the region. The port employs thousands of Moroccans through 750 companies and, in 2017, generated nearly $7 billion in revenue.[17] According to the Maghreb Arab Press, the government's official news agency, in 2018 the port exported goods valued at 139 billion dirhams (which was more than 50% of the country's exports), processed more than 52 million tons of cargo, and handled imports and exports by volume worth more than any other port in Africa.[18] The port also exported nearly 500,000 vehicles in 2018, 80% from the Renault terminal.[19] By 2014, the port was already operating at maximum capacity, just seven years after the project was first opened.

Recognizing the port's early success and its potential for further growth, Mohammed VI and his advisers decided to expand the port and began building Tanger Med II in 2009. Expected to become fully operational in 2019, the port will be able to handle more than eight million 20-foot equivalent units (TEU), two million cars, seven million passengers, and ten million metric tons of oil products, nearly three times the amount the port could handle in 2015.[20] The expansion will make it the largest transshipment hub in the Mediterranean Sea and Africa.[21]

Morocco's other ports – all managed by the National Agency of Ports – handled 83.7 million tons of traffic, an 8% increase from 2016 and a 20% increase from 2010.[22] The majority of the tonnage came from imports (47.7 million tons) compared to the 32.4 million tons in exports and 3.5 million tons of cabotage.[23] The majority of the traffic was from Morocco's trade in phosphates and its derivatives (31.5 million tons), then hydrocarbons (11.2 million tons), and cereals (6.5 million tons).[24] In addition to Tanger Med, the other ports that can handle containers, Casablanca and Agadir, processed 1.19 million TEUs in 2017, a 4% increase compared to the year before and more than 25% since 2010.[25]

The King has invested more than 3 billion dirhams per year in modernizing and expanding the country's seaports since 2008, more than half of which went to the Tanger Med project.[26] According to the Ministry of Equipment, Transport, and Logistic, the National Port Strategy 2030 has identified numerous projects at an estimated cost of $6 billion that will require government and private funding to complete, including the new Atlantic Port of Kenitra ($800 million), Port of Nador West Med ($900 million), Safi Port ($700 million), and Jorf Lasfar Port ($700 million).[27] The investments have not only led to increased opportunities in the maritime industry but also supported the growth of numerous other industries that are able to use the ports to attract investment, including PSA Peugeot Citroen's $650 million investment in a new plant in Kenitra to produce 200,000 cars and 200,000 engines per year.[28]

In addition to commercial projects, the King has invested in marinas to attract tourists and international cruise ships. Despite the investment, however, the number of tourists arriving via cruise liners has continued to drop dramatically. In 2017, only 222,500 passengers arrived into Agadir, Casablanca, and Tanger, the only ports able to receive large cruise ships.[29] This is a 51% drop from 2010[30] and a 34% decrease from the year before.[31] Despite the decline, overall tourism numbers have been steadily increasing for over a decade.[32] The majority of tourists increasingly prefer to travel to Morocco through the Casablanca and Marrakesh airports instead.[33]

Ultimately, the King's investments in the country's seaports have been a major driver of FDI in export-focused industries like aeronautics and automobiles. Renault maintains its own section within the Tanger Med port; PSA Peugeot Citroen was enticed to open its own factory in Kenitra; and other MNCs like Boeing, Bombardier, and Alcoa Aerospace have also relocated or expanded production – all focused mainly on exports. This has also allowed Morocco to become a vital hub for trade around the world. For example, the Tanger Med port now regularly processes millions of tons of transshipments since the port opened, surpassing 30 million tons in 2016.[34]

King Mohammed VI and his economic advisers have also invested heavily in improving the roads and railroads to help facilitate commerce. By decreasing the travel and time associated with transporting goods around the country, the government hoped to entice additional companies to relocate to Morocco as well as to strengthen the competitiveness of local firms. By improving commercial as well as passenger railroads, Moroccan economic planners wanted to demonstrate how advanced Morocco's infrastructure has become and that it was capable of producing and transporting globally the most advanced equipment, but at a fraction of Europe's cost.

Since 2010, the King has invested heavily in improving and expanding the country's roads, nearly 8 billion dirhams per year, including the completion of 1,800 km of highway and 2,500 km of roads across the rural parts of the country.[35] Phosphates, long one of Morocco's most important exports, have regularly been the leading domestic freight by volume, primarily by rail on its way to one of the country's ports. But excluding phosphates, 75% of domestic freight travels across the country's network of roads and accounts for approximately 15 billion dirhams per year in turnover.[36]

The road shipping industry consists of thousands of companies, 95% are SMEs, often just one individual operating one truck.[37] Of that, approximately half of the firms are unregistered and the average truck is 13 years old.[38] This has left the industry outdated and difficult to regulate, creating a challenge for further development. The largest company shipping on the roads is the National Company of Transport and Logistics (SNTL), a public company that was first created in 1937 and operates over 130,000 trucks that transport over 20,000 tons of goods per year valued at approximately 700–900 million dirhams.[39] Other major firms include the following: Carré SMTR, a subsidiary of the state-run railroad company ONCF; Dislog, a private operator that is strong in fast moving consumer goods; and TIMAR, a regional operator with subsidiaries throughout West Africa.

The country has also invested nearly 6 billion dirhams per year since 2010 into its rail network, but still lags in its coverage across the country. Instead of building out the network to support industrial transport more fully, the King invested heavily in a high-speed rail line that connects Casablanca with Tangier. Al Boraq first opened at the end of 2018 and will eventually connect with Marrakesh and Agadir. The $2.3 billion train system is the only high-speed train in Africa and has reduced a five- to six-hour ride to less than two hours.[40] Financial support for the project came from France ($1 billion), Saudi Arabia, Kuwait, and the United Arab Emirates ($500 million) and included new rail lines, train cars, and renovated stations.[41] As one geopolitical analyst told the Guardian, "the government sees this as a flagship project that enables Morocco to shine in Africa," and as such, is designed to show the world, particularly global investors, that Morocco is open for business.[42]

King Mohammed VI highlighted Morocco's rail strategy in a 2015 speech on the 40th anniversary of the Green March, when he said, "We hold the dream of creating a train line from Tangier to La Guera [Western Sahara] to link Morocco to the rest of Africa."[43] Specifically, the strategy hopes to expand conventional lines by 1,600 km and high-speed lines by 1,100 km, double the number of cities and ports the lines connect to, and reach more than three-quarters of the population by 2040.[44] But with so much invested in the high-speed rail line, there is skepticism about its economic feasibility.

The transport of goods via rail has traditionally been dominated by phosphates heading to ports, accounting for nearly two billion dirhams in 2016 (77% of all freight traffic) followed by hydrocarbons and chemicals like acid and sulfur.[45] In addition, the rail system transports containers with a variety of goods to and from ports, most of that traffic going between Casablanca and Marrakesh. However, the increased traffic in Tanger Med has accentuated the importance of an effective and efficient rail network that can foster growth throughout the country.

Despite the King's investments, the new seaports, new roads, and new bullet trains have not resulted in better evaluations by the World Bank's Logistics Performance Index. In particular, the country's infrastructure score dropped 15%, but concerns over customs and tracking explain the majority of the downgrade compared to competitors.[46] Morocco's average score, from 2012 to 2018, places the Kingdom 87 out of 168, ahead of Algeria but behind Egypt.[47] It is not all bad news though, Morocco has consistently scored well on the time and costs associated with importing and exporting goods, better than most in the region including Tunisia and Algeria.[48]

Auto and aeronautics industries

The automotive industry has become one of the most successful within the country and across the region. As of 2017, Morocco's auto industry was the second largest in Africa, behind South Africa, and operated the largest production plant on the continent, capable of assembling 400,000 cars per year.[49] Not only was Morocco able to take advantage of its labor-cost advantage and closeness to Europe, but the King's industrial policy supported the creation of an attractive and burgeoning industry integrated into the global value chain.

Compared to European competitors, Morocco's labor costs make the country an attractive investment. And the country's quick access to European markets, across the Strait of Gibraltar or Mediterranean Sea, offer minimal shipping times compared to other competitors farther from Europe. But without the important initiatives instituted by the King to entice foreign investment, the industry may have never developed into the regional leader it has become.

Morocco's automotive industry began in 1959, when Morocco formed the Société Marocaine de Constructions Automobiles (SOMACA) to produce vehicles for the local market. Although the plurality of the firm was owned by the state (38%), it received technical assistance from European automakers Fiat and Simca, each controlling a 20% stake in the company, in addition to Renault (8%) and private Moroccan citizens (14%).[50] Due to its limited capabilities, SOMACA was producing and selling models of Fiat, Simca, and eventually Renault.[51] By 1968, SOMACA was producing 10,000 cars per year. The state-owned company's production peaked in 1975 at just over 25,000 cars, before seeing a 37% decrease by 1980 when Simca stopped making cars entirely. By the mid-90s, Morocco's automaking industry had almost collapsed. In 1995, SOMACA produced just 8,500 vehicles.[52] But that same year, the government signed an agreement with Fiat that helped resurrect the industry.[53]

In 1970, as a part of the country's import substitution strategy, the government required that at least 40% of the parts and components in a vehicle be produced within Morocco.[54] Although production declined, the initiative allowed for the beginnings of a knowledge transfer to local firms. This proved vital in creating the environment necessary to make the 1995 agreement with

Fiat successful. The agreement lasted only eight years, but led to a number of foreign suppliers moving production to Morocco, which provided critical support to the local suppliers and helped establish new ones, creating the beginnings of Morocco's integration into the global value chain.[55] A year later, the country signed an agreement with Renault and another one with Fiat. By 2009, just over a decade later, production had increased to 90,000 cars per year, including exports to Europe and parts of North Africa.[56]

But in an important achievement for King Mohammed VI and his economic development team, in 2007 the Renault-Nissan Group committed to investing over $1 billion into building its Tangier facility that now produces 400,000 cars per year.[57] Renault had a footprint in Morocco for decades, but its decision to make such a large investment, despite Morocco's limited domestic market, was driven by numerous favorable incentives that the King and his government offered the manufacturer. These included a capped 8.75% tax rate after an initial five-year tax exemption, a reduced value-added tax, subsidized loans from the Hassan II Fund (200 million euros) and three local banks (105 million euros), and 300 hectares of land provided for the facility.[58] Renault's investment ensured Morocco's nascent automotive industry attained the OEM needed to attract additional suppliers to Morocco, a process known as "follow sourcing," and integrate the local industry into the global value chain.[59]

Common within the automotive industry, OEMs like Renault often bring their preferred suppliers with them to new markets which drives demand downstream to third- and fourth-tier suppliers and allows countries to gradually substitute imported parts with local production.[60] Maybe the most successful example within the automotive industry is Mexico, which by 2014 had become the fourth largest exporter of vehicles in the world and developed a high specialization in the sector.[61] In order to create the required environment, not only to attract an OEM but also the necessary first- and second-tier suppliers, Mexico negotiated favorable agreements that included investments in local infrastructure and direct investment incentives.[62] And Mohammed VI's strategy follows Mexico's model; in addition to having a large market to its north, both countries enticed a MNC to invest significant production through a variety of incentives including the provision of land, tax reduction, and training support.

The spread of free trade in the 1980s and 1990s allowed MNCs to expand and relocate their production process – in addition to their final product – around the world.[63] Corporations were able to develop global strategies that sought out the most advantageous deals while also allowing developing countries to enter or upgrade nascent domestic industries. Morocco's King took advantage of this opportunity to a degree unlike others in the region, recognizing the Kingdom's advantages in labor cost (compared to Europe) in addition to its proximity and preferential market access, and by offering transport and logistics that met the needs of foreign producers. At the same time, the King offered generous packages of incentives to foreign companies to convince them to relocate some of their factories to Morocco.

Like the National Energy Plan, the implementation of an extensive industrial plan, including the automotive industry, was crucial in Morocco's development. The 1990s was focused primarily on privatization and saw a decline in trade protections.[64] One of King Mohammed VI's first decisions was to adopt a form of capitalism that suited Morocco. The King moved away from a completely laissez-faire approach and added government incentives to support the country's liberalization policies. In 2000, the King created the Hassan II Fund for Economic and Social Development, which offered companies 15% of their total investment (up to 30 million dirhams) in financial assistance for new buildings and equipment.[65] Then, the government developed the National Pact for Industrial Emergence (NPIE), originally introduced in 2004 as the Emergence Plan. The expansive initiative set out to promote six main industries (offshoring, automotive, aeronautics, electronics, textiles, and food processing) improve the competitiveness of SMEs, strengthen industrial training and education, improve the business climate, and create an agency focused exclusively in promoting foreign investment.[66] That agency was originally called the Moroccan Investment Development Agency and is now called Invest in Morocco.

Within the automotive industry, the NPIE sought to attract more international suppliers and manufacturers by improving the overall conditions, focusing on training programs as the King had required in other targeted sectors, marketing support, and improving the Integrated Industrial Platforms in Tangier and Kenitra that would provide telecommunications, banking, healthcare, logistical, and engineering services.[67] To incentive more firms to create a production facility in Morocco, the country also offered real estate deals.[68] Although the NPIE failed to meet its goal of 400,000 new jobs by the end of 2015, it laid the groundwork, including tax and other incentives, for companies to invest and relocate to the country.[69] By 2012, the NPIE had attracted nearly 8 billion dirhams in FDI, created over 110,000 jobs, increased automotive exports by 125%, and improved the country's infrastructure.[70]

Then in April 2014, the King announced the latest economic development initiative, the Industrial Acceleration Plan (PAI). As a part of the PAI, the government created the Industrial Development Fund and allocated the fund $2.18 billion through 2020.[71] In order to receive support from the fund – up to 20% for real estate or trainings – a company must invest over 50 million dirhams or commit to creating over 200 jobs.[72]

For the automotive industry, the PAI hoped to develop Morocco into a major hub for exports to Europe and further integrate the local industry with the global value chain by expanding production to one million vehicles, increasing the percentage of inputs produced by Moroccan firms to 80%, and employing 165,000 Moroccans.[73] The strategy focused on developing various aspects of production including wiring, vehicle interiors and seats, metal pressing, batteries, bodywork, and motors and transmissions, and incentivized the effort through financial, training, and real estate packages for both local and foreign companies.[74] In addition, Morocco has developed ecosystems that are trying to create better integration and productivity by partnering industry leaders, like a major supplier, with local SMEs looking to expand.[75] Understanding their continued importance to the nascent industry, the PAI also paid special attention on the two largest OEMs, Renault and PSA, in order to ensure their continued success.[76]

Morocco's ecosystems have shifted some of the decision-making process from entirely state led to a more collaborative environment between public and private institutions.[77] Programs like Invest in Morocco and the Moroccan Industry Association for Automotive Producers (AMICA) have worked alongside the firms to address the concerns and needs of the industry. And training programs, including the Institutes for Vocational Training for the Automotive Sector located in Casablanca, Kenitra, and Tangier, have offered Moroccans opportunities to develop the skills necessary to enter the industry.

The efforts of King Mohammed VI have paid off, driving both industrial development and employment in the transportation industry. In 2013, the automotive industry exported more than any other in the Moroccan economy, including phosphates, and drew in over 43% of the total FDI for the entire industrial sector.[78] As a percent of total exports, automotive exports increased from 13.2% in 2008 to 20% in 2015[79] and sales topped 40 billion dirhams by 2014, a 26% increase from the year before.[80] In just under a decade, the country increased production by over 2,000% from 18,500 in 2003 to 400,000 in 2014 and in 2015 the automotive industry was employing 80,000 people.[81]

By increasing production to 800,000 cars, the King hopes to add an additional 90,000 employees and see exports reach 100 billion dirhams by 2020.[82] And by 2018, according to the Ministry of Industry, Trade, Investment and Digital Economy, the automotive industry was increasingly close to their 2020 goals having added 85,000 jobs from 2014 to 2018, reaching 50.5% local integration, and exporting 60 billion dirhams.[83]

Approximately 160 different domestic and international firms, including MNCs Renault, PSA Peugeot-Citroen, and Ford, and at least half a dozen other global suppliers, have production facilities in Morocco.[84] While Renault currently dominates the market, international first-tier suppliers like JTEKT[85] and Nexteer, both multinational producers of steering products, have recently announced plans to open manufacturing facilities in Morocco.[86] In announcing the opening of its plant in March 2018, Hervé Boyer, Nexteer's vice president and chief operating officer, indicated that not only did the company want to extend its reach into southwestern Europe, it considered the "well known...scheme to support foreign investment in Morocco."[87] Boyer also insisted that the company was not there just to provide for Renault and PSA, but to use the plant to supply many of its other customers, including BMW, Fiat Chrysler, Ford, GM, Toyota, and VW.

The plant will be based in Kenitra where a port is expected to be operational by 2022. But the major challenge for Nexteer, according to Boyer, is "to develop the ecosystem when it comes to suppliers" that can support the technology and machining the company relies on.[88] The very ecosystem the King and his ministers have been trying to create through the PAI.

As Nexteer's announcement indicates, access to quality local suppliers can be vital for the success of a multinational firm relocating or expanding into a new market. But it is also important for the domestic industry that local suppliers are capable of partnering with the international firms.[89] In order to achieve export success and sustainability for domestic suppliers, not just from OEMs, firms must be able to progress from low-value products to more sophisticated, high-value products.[90] When local firms do partner with international suppliers, as Nadia Benabdejlil has demonstrated, companies achieve a level of knowledge transfer through formal trainings as well as an informal learning process, particularly developed through relationships.[91]

While the domestic industry remains reliant on labor-intensive production like vehicle assembly and wiring, this may be beginning to change. PSA Peugeot-Citroen's Kenitra plant, which expected to be operational by 2020, has already started producing what will become 200,000 cars and 200,000 engines per year.[92] The engine production will be a first for the country and a potentially significant step into producing more value-added parts and components. The plant is expected to create 5,000 direct jobs from assembly-line laborers to engineers, up to 20,000 indirect local jobs, and provide up to 80% of the parts and components from local suppliers for the cars and engines by 2022, generating at least $1.17 billion.[93]

As Tina Hahn and Georgeta Vidican-Auktor, who have analyzed Morocco's automotive strategies, note,

> in spite of its small market size, Morocco not only attracted foreign direct investment (FDI) in this sector, but also diversified and became more sophisticated in the production process…supported especially by innovative industrial policy practices based on coordination across stakeholders.[94]

Hahn and Vidican-Auktor correctly identify that the government's holistic approach allowed for the automotive industry to emerge as an important regional hub that not only took advantage of its cheaper labor and closeness to European markets but also created the necessary incentives and structures for the industry to achieve success.

Yet in order to ensure the industry's long-term success, one that could withstand an OEM plant relocation or dissolution, the country's domestic firms need to continue to enhance their capabilities toward higher value-added products. Empirical evidence shows that this is occurring,[95] but challenges including the "premature deindustrialization" phenomenon – wherein manufacturing value-added shares in GDP decline earlier and at lower levels of income than developed countries – are found to already be happening in the region and threaten to reverse the country's progress to date.[96] In addition, as Benabdejlil et al. have found that Moroccan firms still lack a thorough integration into the automotive supply chain, in part, because the government's beneficial policies toward foreign firms have reduced the local firm's competitive advantage.[97]

But opportunities remain for Morocco's industry to continue to improve. In 2017, Morocco signed 26 different automotive manufacturing deals worth $1.45 billion.[98] And the car industry is expected to continue to grow in Africa by approximately 8% per year through at least 2025, strengthening the importance of Morocco's location and investment in the country's industry.[99] With one of the lowest motorization rates (44 vehicles per 1,000 inhabitants) in the world, the continent's development will almost certainly result in more car purchases.[100]

And while Moroccan firms that aspire to produce for the automakers may not have achieved the success they desire yet, thousands of Moroccans have already secured jobs and skills in the industry. Further, Morocco's Industrial Acceleration Plan (PAI) which will conclude in 2020 has already begun the work of stimulating Moroccan production for automotives. It, too, has not achieved its ambitious goals, but progress has been made. For example, during the period between 2014 and 2020, the PAI had established the goal of achieving 80% use of local inputs in the automotive industry. According to the Oxford Business Group, as of 2017, the local content of automobiles produced in Morocco was 40%.[101] While this is half the goal that Moroccan planners hoped to achieve, it represents a reliable market for Moroccan producers that previously did not exist.

Like the automotive industry, during the early years of Mohammed VI's reign, the aeronautics industry received specific Moroccan government support and enticed OEMs Boeing and Airbus (formerly EADS) to open factories in Morocco. Boeing's presence in Morocco began in 2001 when it co-founded the Morocco Aero-Technical Interconnect Systems (MATIS) Aerospace in Casablanca to produce engines and parts for Boeing jets.[102] With the King's support, this industry expanded to nearly 100 companies participating in various levels of the global value chain including in production, services, and engineering.[103] Then in 2014, the PAI identified several ecosystems within the aeronautics industry: assembly, electrical wiring, maintenance and repair, and engineering with the hope of creating an environment of support and integration between the major international firms and the local SMEs. The goal has been to add 23,000 new jobs, export 16 billion dirhams, add 100 new firms, and develop 35% local integration by 2020.[104]

In support of these goals, Mohammed VI's government committed 3 billion dirhams per year from 2014 to 2020 through the Industrial Development Fund in order to help firms acquire land (up to 20% of the cost), build external infrastructure (up to 5% of the total investment), and provide vocational training (up to 20%).[105] The government also offers Hassan II Fund grants (up to 15% of the project's total investment and not to exceed 30 million dirhams) and tax exemptions for the first three years for import duties and value-added taxes on capital equipment and materials valued at more than 200 million dirhams.[106] In addition, free trade zones in Tangier, Kenitra, Casablanca, Rabat, and Oujda offer additional incentives including 100% tax exemption during the first five years of operation and a reduced tax rate of 8.75% over the next 25 years.[107] Local SMEs offered support through Maroc PME, as well as Imtiaz Growth, Istitmar Growth, and Auto-Entrepreneur, which all offer financial and tax incentives for new investments.[108]

Since 2011, the Moroccan Aerospace Institute, established by Moroccan Association of Aeronautics and Aerospace (GIMAS) in partnership with the Moroccan government, French Development Agency (a state-run financial institution), and the French Union of Metal Industries, has trained over 1,500 people in composites, sheet metal work, and electronic systems with a 99% hire rate.[109] In addition, with the continuing demand for skilled jobs, Royal Air Maroc, the Moroccan national carrier, partnered with the Bureau of Professional Training and Employment to launch the Specialized Institute for Aeronautics and Airport Logistics and the Specialized Institute of Applied Technology in 2013, to be able to provide training.

The efforts by the Moroccan government in collaboration with the private sector appear to be working. According to the Oxford Business Group, GIMAS "has played a significant role – in collaboration with the public authorities – in shaping the policies that govern the sector."[110] The Moroccan Ministry of Industry, Trade, Investment and Digital Economy has noted that in recent years the industry has shown "outstanding dynamism," particularly as a subcontractor for wiring, mechanics, sheet metal work, composites, and mechanical assembly.[111] By 2018, less than 15 years from its genesis in Morocco, the industry has seen exports double and sales exceed $1.2 billion.[112] In addition, 15,000 have been employed and local integration nearly doubled from 17%[113] in 2016 to 29% in 2018.[114]

In 2012, Bombadier Aerospace announced it would join Boeing and Airbus in Morocco by investing $200 million in a new manufacturing plant that expects to employ 850 by 2020[115] and support 4,400 other indirect jobs.[116] In 2014, Alcoa Aerospace also announced it would be investing in a production facility in the Midparc free trade zone in Casablanca.[117] International firms have also created local subsidiaries like Matis Aerospace, a joint venture between Boeing and Safran, Astema, a subsidiary of Exxelia, and Aerolia and Stelia Aerospace, subsidiaries of Airbus.[118]

Unlike some of the other goals set out in the PAI, Morocco is likely to approach its 2020 aeronautics goals. The industry is not only growing at a rate of 18% per year, the country has already nearly met its export and local integration goals.[119] However, as Benbrahim El Andaloussi, president of the Moroccan Aerospace Institute, noted to the Oxford Business Group, the "key challenge for the aeronautics segment in Morocco is our ability to meet the needs of industry in terms of qualified human resources."[120] While it may not reach 23,000 jobs by 2020, the industry's growth and its investment in training programs promise to continue to deliver increasingly desirable jobs and meet the industry's needs.

King Mohammed VI set out to make Morocco a global trading hub and he and his advisors achieved their goal. The King's investments in the transportation sector – from enhancing its ports, roads, and rail line to attracting MNCs in the automotive and aeronautics industries – has resulted in Morocco having the African continent's largest port, the fastest trains, and the second most productive car industry. The King's interventions in support of private enterprise have proven critical in allowing the transportation sector to thrive and approach many of the country's development goals.

According to the World Bank's 2019 Doing Business report, its annual survey evaluating the ease of doing business in countries around the world, Morocco scored 60 out of 190 countries, second only to the United Arab Emirates among Arab countries and 20 spots higher than its closest North African neighbor.[121] The report identifies several areas where Morocco has continued to improve over the last year, including simplifying the process when starting a business and registering property, as well as improving the border infrastructure for imports and exports.[122] These are clear indicators that the King's efforts are producing results. And they are supported by the Kingdom's strong global rankings for the ease in starting a business (34), dealing with construction permits (18), and paying taxes (25).[123] But the country needs to improve in the ease of getting credit (112), something local businesses have had difficulty with, in particular.[124] For the country's continued development, more government support is needed for local firms, from underwriting local investments to expanding access to high-skilled trainings. While topline growth has produced some jobs, the goals set in the PAI and other national strategies have too often not been met, which has continued to create a gap between the haves and the have-nots in the country. This flared up late in 2018 when the new high-speed train hit someone on its route and ONCF's press release in response frustrated Moroccans who felt the incident reflected an insensitive disregard for the people by the state-owned company.[125]

It appears that the King's development strategies have been betting that the expansion of production, especially by foreign investors, would create more jobs, which, in turn, would improve the lives of Moroccans across the country. But Moroccan leaders need to be cognizant that this process has clearly not occurred as expected, and that more intentional policy planning is required to address the needs of those citizens who have little. It also appears, however, that Morocco's leaders have adopted an energetic program for expanding trade that they also hope will bolster the fortunes of Moroccan workers.

Morocco's trade record

During the initial years of his reign, King Mohammed VI and his advisors focused on making Morocco a focal point for global trade propelled largely by foreign corporations. With the launch in 2014 of the Industrial Acceleration Plan (PAI), the King pivoted to give attention to initiatives for expanding Moroccan production and export in the sectors where the Kingdom had traditional production advantages. These included three industries discussed above – phosphates, aeronautics, and automobiles. But the plan also focused on further modernizing and expanding Morocco's production of agriculture, textiles, and pharmaceuticals.

When King Mohammed VI ascended the throne, Moroccan agriculture was overly dependent on good rains and its access to European states. But Morocco was not a member of the EU and its exports to Europe had to compete with the Southern countries of the EU like Spain, Portugal, Italy, and Greece, that grew many of the same food products that Morocco produced. European consumers had to pay higher prices for Moroccan goods since Morocco was outside Europe's (common) market and Moroccan producers did not receive the subsidies that EU producers received through the EU's Common Agricultural Policy (CAP). Moreover, the EU's CAP stipulated that many Moroccan goods that competed with EU members could not even enter the EU except during limited times when EU producers could not deliver their products to market.

For many years, King Hassan II and King Mohammed VI believed that Morocco eventually would be invited to join the EU. But at the EU's historic meeting in 1993, the organization adopted the Copenhagen criteria for membership: only countries that were stable democracies and respected human rights would be admitted. Hassan II's Morocco was neither a democracy nor respectful of human rights. When Mohammed VI began his reign in 1999, the EU was busy with the business of integrating new countries from the former Soviet bloc and gave little attention to Morocco or other Southern Mediterranean country requests for membership.

Yet, despite the challenges, Moroccan trade with EU countries grew ($5,448 million in 1999 to $8,203 million in 2009). And almost a decade into Mohammed VI's rule, in 2008, Morocco entered into an "advanced status" with the EU following long negotiations. Though this advanced status did not have a widespread effect on Morocco's agricultural sector which is a major employer of Moroccan labor. And unfortunately, many Moroccan young people want to head to the cities. So the King has been challenged by both external and internal factors in trying to expand Morocco's agricultural trade.

In 2003, young Moroccan terrorists planted and exploded bombs in Casablanca, shocking the nation. As James Sater's research has demonstrated, for a time, the attacks focused Morocco's leaders on the issues of poverty and on the migration of Moroccan youth from the rural areas to Morocco's urban ghettos.[126] The government produced poverty maps and launched the National Initiative for Human Development, but, as Sater argues, local journalists claimed that there was only an increase in development projects with little oversight for the quality or the integration of such projects into larger development plans.[127] Likewise, Paul Rivlin's work demonstrates that Morocco's working age population was continuing to increase during the first decade of King Mohammed VI's reign even though it was the lowest increase when compared to other Middle East and North Africa countries.[128] As of January 2019, Morocco's youth unemployment rate stood at 26%.[129] Unemployed youth migrating from rural to urban areas remains an unsolved problem for Morocco's development planners.

The year 2008 ushered in a global economic crisis for all countries. So, it is important to note that also in 2008, Morocco created the Plan Maroc Vert (PMV) in order to restructure and support its agricultural sector. PMV targeted both large commercial agriculture and smallholder farms in rural Morocco. Simultaneously in 2008, Morocco developed its Industrial Acceleration Plan (PAI) which targeted the promotion of food processing in order to add value to Morocco's food exports and earn more in global markets. And, as in other sectors, the King and his advisors realized that more training was needed in Morocco's agricultural sector and so vocational training also became part of Morocco's agricultural planning.

Because Morocco's agricultural sector employs about 75% of its labor force, creating protection against drought, increasing its production, and finding markets for its goods are critical to distributing the benefits of Moroccan development across the country.

Moroccan production of textiles employs fewer workers than its agricultural sector but textiles have long been a component of Morocco's exports and the sector was believed to be an area in which Morocco could expand. The Industrial Acceleration Plan 2014–2020 set a goal of increasing Moroccan jobs in the textile sector to 100,000.[130]

Morocco's fortunes in this sector are driven by both consumer demand in target countries, especially in Europe (which, in turn, depends on the health of the economies in those countries), and by competition from ready-made garments coming from China and other late industrializing states. But textiles also are dependent on fashion trends.

Through excellent development planning and through private sector innovations, Morocco has managed to adapt its textile sector to compete in the ready-made garment sector. And Morocco's new ports that move freight quickly combined with its geographical closeness to Europe has allowed Morocco to switch its production as fashion changes and compete in European markets. Morocco's textile exports have increased from about $3.6 billion in 2015 to about $4 billion in 2017.[131]

To make Morocco's pharmaceutical sector more competitive and also able to service the domestic market more effectively, the 2014 Industrial Acceleration Plan encouraged Moroccan officials to shorten the certification process in the country for new medications.[132] Morocco already produces many of the medicines required on its domestic market but Moroccan development planners hoped to expand production at home and also to increase exports.

Unfortunately, one of the drawbacks for this expansion is Morocco's dependence on producers from other countries for the active ingredients needed in its products.[133] While the country has made some progress in expanding success, the pharmaceutical sector is not a sector that has accomplished it goals.

During King Mohammed VI's 20 years of reign, Morocco has made outstanding progress in its transportation sector, including ports, trains, roads, shipping, and aeronautics. These industries, however, have relied heavily on foreign investment and foreign technical skills. It is critical now that Morocco begins to emphasize more support for local businesses. Additionally, Morocco needs to create domestic linkages within the country and build its domestic demand for goods and services. This will not only attract more foreign investors who see an opportunity to increase sales within Morocco, in addition to using the country as a hub for exports but also help to insulate the country from its vulnerability in the global economy.

Notes

1 Ali, A. A., & Msadfa, Y. (2016, April). *Industrial Policy, Structural Change and Global Value Chains Participation: Case study of Morocco, Tunisia and Egypt* (Rep.). Retrieved February 2018 from OCP Policy Center website: http://www.policycenter.ma/sites/default/files/PP 16-04_0.pdf (p. 23).
2 *Manufacturing Industry Central to Morocco's Exports.* (2018, July 3). Retrieved from https://oxfordbusinessgroup.com/overview/new-ecosystem-manufacturing-becoming-central-kingdom's-exports.
3 *Industrial Acceleration Plan 2014–2020.* (n.d.). Retrieved from Royaume du Maroc Ministere de I'Industrie, de I'Investissement, du Commerce et de I'Economie Numerique: http://www.mcinet.gov.ma/en/content/industrial-acceleration-plan-2014-2020-0.
4 Ibid.
5 Ibid.
6 Ibid.
7 Ibid.
8 El Mokri, K. (2016, November). *Morocco's 2014–2020 Industrial Strategy and Its Potential Implications for the Structural Transformation Process* (Rep.). Retrieved May 2018 from OCP Policy Center website: http://www.policycenter.ma/sites/default/files/OCPPC-PB1627vEn.pdf (p. 3).
9 Rensma, M., & Hamoumi, S. (2018, May). *Business Opportunities Dutch Companies in Transport & Logistics Sector Morocco* (Rep.). Retrieved January 2019 from Ministry of Foreign Affairs, Netherlands website: https://www.rvo.nl/sites/default/files/2018/05/Transport-and-Logistics-sector-Morocco.pdf (pp. 60–61).
10 Ibid., p. 61.
11 Ibid., p. 31.
12 Ibid.
13 Ibid., p. 32.
14 Ibid., p. 33.
15 Ibid.
16 Ibid.
17 *Morocco's Tanger-Med Port Running at Full Speed.* (2018, April 4). Retrieved from https://www.news24.com/Africa/News/moroccos-tanger-med-port-running-at-full-speed-20180404.

18 *Tangier Med Port Handles 50% of All Moroccan Exports.* (2019, February 05). Retrieved from https://www.moroccoworldnews.com/2019/02/265084/tangier-med-port-moroccan-exports/.

19 Ibid.

20 *Tangier Med II.* (n.d.). Retrieved January 20, 2019, from https://www.besix.com/en/projects/tangier-med-ii.

21 Saleh, H. (2016, March 23). *Morocco's Tanger-Med Container Port Provides Bridge to Europe.* Retrieved from https://www.ft.com/content/59139520-cb3f-11e5-a8ef-ea66e967dd44.

22 *ANP Annual Report 2017* (Rep.). (2017). Retrieved January 2019 from National Agency of Ports website: https://www.anp.org.ma/En/Agency/RapportsAnnuel/rapport_En_2017.pdf (p. 12).

23 Ibid., p. 12.

24 Ibid., p. 14.

25 Ibid., p. 13.

26 *Business Opportunities Dutch Companies in Transport & Logistics Sector Morocco,* p. 45.

27 El Amrani, S. (2016). *2030 National Port Strategy* [Brochure]. Retrieved January 2019 from http://docplayer.net/48503294-2030-national-port-strategy-morocco.html (p. 9).

28 Sigal, P. (2018, July 3). *Morocco Gave PSA New Solutions for Building Sales and Exports.* Retrieved from https://europe.autonews.com/article/20180727/COPY/307139992/morocco-gave-psa-new-solutions-for-building-sales-and-exports.

29 *ANP Annual Report 2017,* p. 14.

30 Rensma, M., & Hamoumi, S. (2018, May). *Business Opportunities Dutch Companies in Transport & Logistics Sector Morocco,* p. 46.

31 *ANP Annual Report 2017,* p. 14.

32 *Tourists Arrivals.* (n.d.). Retrieved January 15, 2019, from https://www.tourisme.gov.ma/en/node/3583.

33 Ibid.

34 Rensma, M., & Hamoumi, S. (2018, May). *Business Opportunities Dutch Companies in Transport & Logistics Sector Morocco,* p. 33.

35 *Strategy of the Ministry of Equipment and Transport.* (n.d.). Retrieved February 1, 2019, from http://www.equipement.gov.ma/en/Pages/home.aspx.

36 Rensma, M., & Hamoumi, S. (2018, May). *Business Opportunities Dutch Companies in Transport & Logistics Sector Morocco,* p. 48.

37 Ibid.

38 Ibid.

39 *SNTL Group.* (n.d.). Retrieved February 1, 2019, from http://sntlgroup.ma/home/sntl-group/.

40 Jacobs, H. (2019, January 27). *I Rode Africa's First Superfast Bullet Train That Could Go from New York to Washington, DC, in 90 Minutes, and I Understand Why It's Controversial.* Retrieved February 8, 2019, from https://www.businessinsider.com/bullet-train-africa-morocco-casablanca-tangier-2019-1.

41 Ibid.

42 Doig, W. (2018, December 13). *Will Africa's First High-Speed Train Be a £1.5bn Magic Bullet for Morocco?* Retrieved February 8, 2019, from https://www.theguardian.com/global-development/2018/dec/13/africa-high-speed-train-magic-bullet-morocco.

43 *Plan Rail Maroc.* (n.d.). Retrieved February 1, 2019, from https://www.oncf.ma/en/Development/Strategy/Morroco-s-2040-rail-strategy.

44 Ibid.

45 Rensma, M., & Hamoumi, S. (2018, May). *Business Opportunities Dutch Companies in Transport & Logistics Sector Morocco,* p. 59.

46 Arvis, J., Ojala, L., Wiederer, C., Shepherd, B., Raj, A., Dairabayeva, K., & Kiiski, T. (2018). *Connecting to Compete 2018 Trade Logistics in the Global Economy: The Logistics Performance Index and Its Indicators* (Rep.). Retrieved from https://openknowledge.worldbank.org/bitstream/handle/10986/29971/LPI2018.pdf.
47 Ibid.
48 Ibid.
49 Black, A., Makundi, B., & McLennan, T. (2017, September). *Africa's Automotive Industry: Potential and Challenges* (Working paper No. 282). Retrieved from https://www.afdb.org/fileadmin/uploads/afdb/Documents/Publications/WPS_No_282_Africa's_Automotive_Industry_Potential_and_Challenges.pdf (p. 8).
50 DEPF (Direction des Etudes et des Prévisions Financières). (2015). *Le secteur automobile au Maroc: Vers unmeilleur positionnement dans la chaine de valeur mondiale*. Ministère de l'Economie et des Finances. Retrieved from http://www.finances.gov.ma/Docs/2015/DEPF/Note%20automobile.pdf (p. 19).
51 Ibid., p. 20.
52 *Prenez la route avec la banque "toutes options"* (Rep.). (2012). Retrieved from http://www.attijariwafabank.com/Actualites/ALAUNE/Documents/Book_salonautoexpo2012.pdf.
53 Hahn, T., & Vidican-Auktor, G. (2017). *The Effectiveness of Morocco's Industrial Policy in Promoting a National Automotive Industry* (Working paper No. 27). Retrieved from https://www.die-gdi.de/en/discussion-paper/article/the-effectiveness-of-moroccos-industrial-policy-in-promoting-a-national-automotive-industry/ (p. 16).
54 *Prenez la route avec la banque "toutes options"* (Rep.). (2012).
55 Hahn, T., & Vidican-Auktor, G. (2017). *The Effectiveness of Morocco's Industrial Policy in Promoting a National Automotive Industry*, p. 16.
56 *Prenez la route avec la banque "toutes options"* (Rep.). (2012).
57 Haddach, A., Ben Allal, L., Laglaoui, A., & Ammari, M. (2017). *Moroccan Automotive Industry: Opportunities and Perspectives. American Journal of Engineering Research*, 6(8), 75–82. Retrieved from http://www.ajer.org/papers/v6(08)/K06087582.pdf (p. 76).
58 Benabdejlil, N., Lung, Y., & Piveteau, A. (2016). *L'émergence d'un pôle automobile à Tanger (Maroc)* (Rep. No. 4). Retrieved from http://cahiersdugretha.u-bordeaux4.fr/2016/2016-04.pdf (p. 4).
59 Humphrey, J., & Memedovic, O. (2003). *The Global Automotive Industry Value Chain: What Prospects for Upgrading by Developing Countries* (UNIDO Sectorial Studies Series Working Paper). Retrieved from http://papers.ssrn.com/sol3/Papers.cfm?abstract_id=424560 (p. 60).
60 Ibid., p. 22.
61 OECD (Organization for Economic Co-operation and Development). (2016, November 10–11). *Upgrading Pathways in the Automotive Value Chain*. OECD Initiative for Policy Dialogue on Global Value Chains, Production Transformation and Development. 7th Plenary Meeting, Mexico City. Retrieved from http://www.oecd.org/dev/Upgrading-pathways-in-the-automotive-value-chain.pdf (p. 7).
62 Hahn, T., & Vidican-Auktor, G. (2017). *The Effectiveness of Morocco's Industrial Policy in Promoting a National Automotive Industry*, p. 5.
63 Gereffi, G., Humphrey, J., & Sturgeon, T. (2005). The Governance of Global Value Chains. *Review of International Political Economy*, 12 (1), 78–104. doi:10.1080/09692290500049805 (pp. 95–97).
64 Ali, A. A., & Msadfa, Y. (2016, April). *Industrial Policy, Structural Change and Global Value Chains Participation: Case study of Morocco, Tunisia and Egypt*, p. 3.
65 *Business Climate: Hassan II Fund*. (n.d.). Retrieved February 8, 2019, from http://www.invest.gov.ma/index.php?Id=34490&lang=en.

66 JICA (Agence Japonaise de Coopération Internationale). (2014). *Étude pour le développement du secteur privéau royaume du Maroc.* Retrieved from http://open_jicareport.jica.go.jp/pdf/12150686.pdf (p. 1).
67 Hahn, T., & Vidican-Auktor, G. (2017). *The Effectiveness of Morocco's Industrial Policy in Promoting a National Automotive Industry*, p. 22.
68 Ibid., p. 22.
69 Chauffour, Jean-Pierre. 2018. *Morocco 2040: Emerging by Investing in Intangible Capital. Directions in Development—Countries and Regions.* Washington, DC: World Bank. Retrieved from https://openknowledge.worldbank.org/handle/10986/28442 License: CC BY 3.0 IGO, (p. 145).
70 *National Pact for Industrial Emergence.* (n.d.). Retrieved January 20, 2019, from https://www.finances.gov.ma/en/pages/stratégies/pacte-national-pour-l'emergence-industrielle.aspx?m=Investors&m2=Investments.
71 *New Industrial Policy in Morocco Stimulating Growth in Many Segments.* (2015, September 16). Retrieved February 1, 2019, from https://oxfordbusinessgroup.com/overview/new-industrial-policy-morocco-stimulating-growth-many-segments.
72 *Business Climate: Investment and Industrial Development Fund.* (n.d.). Retrieved February 8, 2019, from http://www.invest.gov.ma/index.php?Id=34489&lang=en.
73 Hahn, T., & Vidican-Auktor, G. (2017). *The Effectiveness of Morocco's Industrial Policy in Promoting a National Automotive Industry*, p. 24.
74 *AUTOMOTIVE.* (n.d.). Retrieved February 13, 2019, from http://www.mcinet.gov.ma/en/content/automotive.
75 Hahn, T., & Vidican-Auktor, G. (2017). *The Effectiveness of Morocco's Industrial Policy in Promoting a National Automotive Industry*, p. 23.
76 *AUTOMOTIVE.* (n.d.). Retrieved February 13, 2019, from http://www.mcinet.gov.ma/en/content/automotive.
77 Hahn, T., & Vidican-Auktor, G. (2017). *The Effectiveness of Morocco's Industrial Policy in Promoting a National Automotive Industry*, p. 35.
78 *Le secteur automobile au Maroc: Vers unmeilleur positionnement dans la chaine de valeur mondiale*, pp. 10–11.
79 Hahn, T., & Vidican-Auktor, G. (2017). *The Effectiveness of Morocco's Industrial Policy in Promoting a National Automotive Industry*, p. 2.
80 *New Industrial Policy in Morocco Stimulating Growth in Many Segments.* (2015, September 16).
81 Hahn, T., & Vidican-Auktor, G. (2017). *The Effectiveness of Morocco's Industrial Policy in Promoting a National Automotive Industry*, p. 24.
82 *New Industrial Policy in Morocco Stimulating Growth in Many Segments.* (2015, September 16).
83 *AUTOMOTIVE.* (n.d.). Retrieved February 13, 2019, from http://www.mcinet.gov.ma/en/content/automotive.
84 Office des Changes. (2013). L'industrie automobile au Maroc. Performance à l'export. Retrieved from http://www.oc.gov.ma/portal/sites/default/files/nouvelles%20publications%20statistiques/Etude%20sur%20l'industrie%20automobile%20au%20Maroc.pdf (p. 7).
85 *JTEKT to Establish New EPS Systems Facility in Morocco.* (2017). Aroq - Just-Auto.Com (Global News), 1. Retrieved from http://search.ebscohost.com.proxy1.library.jhu.edu/login.aspx?direct=true&db=bsu&AN=124498103&site=ehost-live&scope=site.
86 Warburton, S. (2018). *New Nexteer Morocco Plant to Aid South Europe Capacity.* Aroq - Just-Auto.Com (Global News), 1. Retrieved from http://search.ebscohost.com.proxy1.library.jhu.edu/login.aspx?direct=true&db=bsu&AN=129022214&site=ehost-live&scope=site.
87 Ibid.
88 Ibid.

89 Ali, A. A., & Msadfa, Y. (2016, April). *Industrial Policy, Structural Change and Global Value Chains Participation: Case Study of Morocco, Tunisia and Egypt*, pp. 19–22.
90 Ibid.
91 Benabdeljlil, N. (2013). *Apprendre dans un réseau: le cas inédit d'un fournisseur automobile marocain. Annales des Mines - Gérer et comprendre*, 112(2), 55–65. doi:10.3917/geco.112.0055.
92 Sigal, P. (2018, July 03). *Morocco Gave PSA New Solutions for Building Sales and Exports.* Retrieved from https://europe.autonews.com/article/20180727/COPY/307139992/morocco-gave-psa-new-solutions-for-building-sales-and-exports.
93 Ibid.
94 Hahn, T., & Vidican-Auktor, G. (2017). *The Effectiveness of Morocco's Industrial Policy in Promoting a National Automotive Industry*, p. 1.
95 Achy, L. (2013, November). *Structural Transformation and Industrial Policy in Morocco* (Working paper No. 796). Retrieved from https://ideas.repec.org/p/erg/wpaper/796.html (p. 6).
96 Rodrik, D. (2015, February). *Premature Deindustrialization* (Working paper No. 20935). Retrieved from https://www.nber.org/papers/w20935.pdf.
97 Benabdeljlil, N., Lung, Y., & Piveteau, A. (2016). *L'émergence d'un pôle automobile à Tanger (Maroc)*, p. 20.
98 *In Numbers: Africa's Automotive Industry.* (2018). *African Business*, (450), 16–17. Retrieved from http://search.ebscohost.com.proxy1.library.jhu.edu/login.aspx?direct=true&db=bsu&AN=128685662&site=ehost-live&scope=site.
99 Ibid.
100 Ibid.
101 "Indicators." *Global Economic Data, Indicators, Charts & Forecasts.* Retrieved April 22, 2018, from https://www.ceicdata.com/en/indicator/morocco/motor-vehicle-production. "Manufacturing Industry Central to Morocco's Exports." Oxford Business Group. March 8, 2018. Accessed April 21, 2018.
102 "Morocco and Boeing Announce Major Aerospace Investment Ahead of Third Annual US-Morocco Business Forum" Moroccan American Center for Policy. September 27, 2016. Retrieved from http://www.marketwired.com/press-release/morocco-boeing-announce-major-aerospace-investment-ahead-third-annual-us-morocco-business-2161976.htm.
103 Ali, A. A., & Msadfa, Y. (2016, April). *Industrial Policy, Structural Change and Global Value Chains Participation: Case Study of Morocco, Tunisia and Egypt*, p. 4.
104 *AERONAUTICS.* (n.d.). Retrieved February 20, 2019, from http://www.mcinet.gov.ma/en/content/aeronautics. Additionally, it is important to note that the grounding of Boeing planes (in 2013 and in 2019), due to overheated batteries and wiring, demonstrates Morocco's vulnerability to global market forces.
105 Ibid.
106 Ibid.
107 *Aeronautical Industry Growing in Morocco.* (2015, September 16). Retrieved February 8, 2019, from https://oxfordbusinessgroup.com/analysis/aeronautical-industry-growing-morocco.
108 *AERONAUTICS.* (n.d.). Retrieved February 20, 2019, from http://www.mcinet.gov.ma/en/content/aeronautics.
109 *Aeronautical Industry Growing in Morocco.* (2015, September 16).
110 Ibid.
111 *AERONAUTICS.* (n.d.). Retrieved February 20, 2019, from http://www.mcinet.gov.ma/en/content/aeronautics.
112 Ibid.

113 *Manufacturing Industry Central to Morocco's Exports.* (2018, July 3). Retrieved February 8, 2019, from https://oxfordbusinessgroup.com/overview/new-ecosystem-manufacturing-becoming-central-kingdom's-exports.
114 *AERONAUTICS.* (n.d.). Retrieved February 20, 2019, from http://www.mcinet.gov.ma/en/content/aeronautics.
115 *Bombardier Aerospace to Establish Its Moroccan Facility in the Greater Casablanca Region.* (n.d.). Retrieved January 18, 2019, from https://www.bombardier.com/en/media/newsList/details.36282-bombardier-aerospace-to-establish-its-moroccan-facility-in-the-greater-casablanca-region.bombardiercom.html.
116 *AERONAUTICS.* (n.d.). Retrieved February 20, 2019, from http://www.mcinet.gov.ma/en/content/aeronautics.
117 *Aeronautical Industry Growing in Morocco.* (2015, September 16).
118 Ibid.
119 *AERONAUTICS.* (n.d.). Retrieved February 20, 2019, from http://www.mcinet.gov.ma/en/content/aeronautics.
120 *Benbrahim El Andaloussi, President, Institut des Métiers de l'Aéronautique* (IMA): Interview. (2018, July 03). Retrieved January 18, 2019, from https://oxfordbusinessgroup.com/interview/steady-climb-benbrahim-el-andaloussi-president-institut-des-métiers-de-l'aéronautique-ima-successful.
121 *Doing Business 2019: Training for Reform* (Rep. No. 16). (2019). Retrieved http://www.worldbank.org/content/dam/doingBusiness/media/Annual-Reports/English/DB2019-report_web-version.pdf.
122 Ibid.
123 Ibid.
124 Ibid.
125 *'This Is Morocco': Despite Grand Development Projects, Problems Persist.* (2018, December 30). Retrieved from https://www.moroccoworldnews.com/2018/12/261978/morocco-development-projects-al-boraq/.
126 Sater, J. N. (2016). *Morocco Challenges to Tradition and Modernity* (London and New York: Routledge).
127 Ibid., p. 136.
128 Rivlin, P. (2013). "Morocco's Economy under Mohammed VI" in Bruce Maddy-Weitzman and Daniel Zisenwine, eds. *Contemporary Morocco* (London and New York: Routledge), p. 82.
129 "Moroccan Youth Unemployment Rate" Trading Economics. Retrieved from https://tradingeconomics.com/morocco/youth-unemployment-rate.
130 "TEXTILE." Ministère De L'Industrie, Du Commerce, De L'Investissement Et De L'Economie Numérique. Retrieved from http://www.mcinet.gov.ma/en/content/textile.
131 Morocco Office of Changes. Foreign Trade Statistics 2016/2017 as quoted in Oberlin Research Group, *Morocco's Grand Sectoral Development Strategies: Logistics, Exports, Solar, and Tourism* (May 2018) hardcopy. p. 10.
132 Oberlin Research Group, *Morocco's Grand Sectoral Development Strategies: Logistics, Exports, Solar, and Tourism* (May 2018) hardcopy.
133 Ibid. This paragraph relies on the work of the Oberlin Research Group's research in this document.

5 Becoming a global leader in renewable energy

Morocco lacks a domestic supply of traditional fossil fuels to meet the country's energy needs, relying on imports to fuel the country. Since 1980, Morocco has imported at least 80% of the country's energy consumption. By 1999, when Mohammed VI ascended the throne, the Kingdom was importing over 90%,[1] which peaked in 2008 at 98%.[2] At the same time, the country's energy infrastructure was not able to meet the growing demand for more energy leading to roaming blackouts.

Meanwhile, the reliance on imports has risked the security of the state and left the country's development exposed to the cost increases in global energy prices. For example, the rise in prices caused fuel subsidies to reach 6.6% of gross domestic product (GDP) in 2012, pushed public debt to 60% of GDP, and diminished foreign reserves to four months' worth of imports of goods and services.[3] Making matters worse, the country has increasingly suffered the effects of climate change, further hurting the country's global competitiveness and burdening the state budget with an increased need for relief, mitigation, and adaptation funds.

When King Mohammed VI ascended the throne, the government knew it had a myriad of problems it needed to address. The country had to improve the existing legislation, permit independent power producers (IPPs), reduce its reliance on imports, adopt improved technologies to enhance efficiency and mitigate the effects to the environment, promote conservation strategies, and increase the capacity of power generation.[4] However, it took another decade before the King began to fully implement these reforms. In 2008, he announced the National Energy Strategy (NES), which continued to embrace liberalization, but selectively intervened to support the sector's growth. In particular, the country took a leapfrog strategy to adopt the latest technological capabilities that would not only reduce the country's energy dependence but also address its climate vulnerabilities.

The demand for energy

From 1985 to 1992, GDP was averaging growth of over 4% per year, but the growth also led to a 6.2% increase per year in electricity usage.[5] The increased demand for energy to sustain and expand the growth was not available, which led to power shortages, roaming blackouts, and costing the country 1% of GDP.[6] According to the World Bank, the energy sector was struggling with power supply issues with an installed energy capacity of 2,220 megawatts (MW) and experiencing numerous problems, including financial shortfalls, lack of autonomy in setting prices, too many institutions overseeing its administration, failure to adjust tariff levels regularly, and an overstretched subsidy regime.[7]

Morocco's continuing demand for energy has coincided with its economic development. Mega-projects, enhanced infrastructure, urbanization, and rural electrification have all driven growth but also increased energy demand. The more the country grows, the more energy it needs. But increased demand has also meant increased subsidy expenditures. In Morocco, fuel subsidies initially began in the early 1940s for liquefied petroleum gas, but they have been a significant part of economic policy throughout the region for decades.[8] According to the International Monetary Fund (IMF), in 2011 more than 75% of the subsidies allocated in the Middle East and North Africa went toward fuel, costing governments $160 billion or 5.5% of the region's GDP.[9]

For Morocco, the government's extensive use of subsidies in the past three decades was driven, in part, by the rural electrification program initiated in 1996. At the time, the country's electrification rate was only 18%.[10] But in order to make access affordable – particularly for poorer rural areas – King Hassan II began subsidizing the cost of electricity and King Mohammed VI continued the practice. The program worked, and by 2015 the electrification rate across the country had reached 99% in both urban and rural areas, leading to more than 12 million new users.[11] However, this also meant millions of additional citizens were now receiving government fuel subsidies. Then, in an effort to help calm the unrest from the February 20th protests that spread through the spring of 2011, the King increased fuel subsidies even more.[12]

The increasing fiscal burden that fuel subsidies were placing on the country was apparent even before the Arab Spring. But in 2012, as a part of a $6.2 billion Precautionary and Liquidity Line (PLL) loan from the IMF to help the country protect against fluctuations in oil prices, the government committed to implement subsidy reform.[13] By 2015, fuel subsidies had been mostly phased out, though as noted above, electricity continued to expand reaching nearly all Moroccans. The Kingdom's success in eliminating its energy subsidies led the international community to tout the success of the King's reform as an important step to reduce the country's debt.[14] Throughout the region though, austerity measures imposed by international financial institutions (IFIs), like the IMF and the World Bank, have often caused civil unrest as citizens express frustration over price increases.

The Kingdom, however, benefited from the concurrent drop in crude oil prices, which lessened the financial impact on Moroccans and helped stave off a larger public response.[15] The King also chose not to cut subsidies for butane gas that is used throughout Morocco for cooking.[16] With its budget a little freer, the government has even considered shifting many of these subsidies toward the cost of electricity from solar power, especially for the expensive concentrated solar power (CSP) projects that still lack economic competitiveness compared to coal.[17]

Another factor driving the increased consumption of energy and fossil fuels in Morocco is the increasing urbanization of the country. Sixty percent of the population now lives within city limits and the rate of urbanization has continued to increase by more than 2% per year.[18] Pushing Moroccans toward the city has been a lack of opportunity and jobs in rural communities outside of the agricultural sector, where 80% of the rural population works.[19]

Agricultural work is tiring, pays little, and with limited other opportunities, young people are heading to the cities to try to find other kinds of work. Making matters worse, the effects of climate change have negatively impacted the farming industry. Of the cultivated agricultural land (12% of the country's total land area), only 13% is irrigated and as bigger storms and longer droughts ruin crop cultivation, more Moroccans will continue to enter cities looking for opportunities.[20] The move from the countryside to the city has changed consumption patterns, including a greater need for transportation and household appliances. It has also changed the consumer's type of energy used, from more traditional biomass products like firewood and charcoal to the city's power grid.

The other major driver of energy consumption comes from the increased commercial energy consumption, which has increased from 10.5 million tons of oil equivalent (TOE) in 2002 to 19.1 million TOE in 2014, or 5.1% annual growth and almost five times the rate of population growth.[21] While Morocco's energy consumption is not exceptional compared to other countries in the region, its reliance on imports leaves the country vulnerable to rising energy prices. Businesses need reliable energy and consistent prices in order to compete in the global marketplace, but with subsidies eliminated their exposure to price fluctuations is greater than their regional competitors. Meanwhile, demands for energy are likely to continue to grow as urbanization, industrialization, and economic growth continue.

Climate change

Morocco was identified by the 4th Assessment Report of the United Nations Intergovernmental Panel on Climate Change (IPCC) as already affected by and at risk of increases in average temperatures, droughts, heat waves, changing rainfall patterns, sea-level rise, and floods.[22] The United Nations has also identified water stress, land degradation, and various types of pollution as areas of concern, much of which is caused by economic activities according to the UN, including production of phosphoric acid, fertilizers, and concentrated minerals; heavy use of pesticides and fertilizers in agriculture; and pharmaceuticals and processing industries.[23] The changing rainfall patterns and increased floods and droughts come at a particular cost since so much of the country's employment (40%) and GDP (14%) come from agriculture, which is particularly vulnerable to these types of climate fluctuations and extreme weather events.[24]

In particular, Morocco has seen the important spring rainfall necessary for cereal crops decrease by 47%, the duration of dry periods increase by 15 days, and the average temperature across the country increase by one degree Celsius since the 1960s.[25] Projection models show these trends continuing to get worse, with expectations of growing desertification, beach erosion, and water scarcity, which are all likely to lead to further displacement, urbanization, and almost certainly hinder economic development. As Meriem Houzir, Mustapha Mokass, and Liane Schalatek have argued, "climate change and Morocco's response to climate change will be major determinants of Morocco's future development options, including addressing social inequities and poverty, which remain despite Morocco's remarkable track record on growth and development."[26]

Although the country's geographic location makes it particularly vulnerable to the effects of climate change, in recent years the steps taken to address its exposure has been significant. By embracing a leapfrog approach in the energy sector, the King has begun to decrease the country's foreign dependency, increase the energy supply, and reduce its climate vulnerabilities. As a result, Morocco is seen as a global leader in combating climate change. Not only has Morocco rated as a top ten best performer in the Climate Change Performance Index (CCPI) since 2015, it was the only developing country in the top 20 through 2017, and remains the only country in the top ten in the 2019 index.[27] In explaining why Morocco jumped six spots in 2015, the index noted, "the kingdom has not only adopted ambitious renewable energy targets, but also supported its commitment with an increasing number of solar and wind projects as means to secure climate-compatible development."[28]

For the 2019 CCPI, Morocco received its highest ranking yet (fifth) just below Sweden. The index commended the country's "consultative process of developing a long-term strategy for 2050," which, "could make the country a policy frontrunner on the international level."[29] Meanwhile, in 2018, Ernst & Young rated Morocco the 15th most attractive country in the world for renewable energy in its annual index.[30] In part, this reflects the government's commitment to investing $40 billion through 2030 in the country's energy sector, 75% of which will be devoted to renewable energy projects.[31]

In addition to the clear environmental need, the King's decision to convert the energy sector toward renewables is both a recognition of Morocco's comparative advantage – due to the prevalence of sunny days and wind off the coast and through its mountains – and the international interest in funding renewable energy projects. The King has embraced this challenge and created an ambitious and strategic plan to develop Morocco's energy sector to meet the growing needs of its citizens.

Sufian Eltayeb Mohamed and Moise G. Sidiropoulos have noted that the prevalence of natural resources has been a strong determinant in driving foreign direct investment (FDI) in countries in the Middle East and North Africa.[32] And Ramon Mahia et al. have demonstrated that attracting FDI for renewable energy benefits from, in addition to the available natural resources, economic stability, openness to trade and investment, a good business environment, and institutional stability.[33] Meanwhile, Kerstin Fritzsche et al. identified five key areas necessary to develop successful renewable energy: policy, financing, knowledge, infrastructure, and partnership, which the King has incorporated into Morocco's energy strategy.[34]

And so far the country's response has led to a decrease in the percentage of energy imported for the first time in decades and an increase in the contribution from renewable energy even though energy consumption has continued to increase. In part, this has been achieved by doubling the renewable energy output from 2002 to 2017 to 5.8% of total consumption, with trend lines showing continued progress on both dependence and contributions from renewable energy.[35] By 2015, total installed energy capacity had increased over 250% to 8,160 MW, with plans to nearly double capacity to 16,000 MW by 2020 and add an additional 10,000 MW by 2030.[36]

Morocco's plan

In order to address its import dependency and vulnerable climate, the King developed a broad, forward-thinking leapfrog strategy that has begun to return positive results. Understanding the country had a natural advantage with an abundance of renewable energy potential, Mohammed VI committed to developing a nearly non-existent renewable energy sector, rather than relying on fossil fuel exploration and importation. First, he established laws to support the renewable energy sector, then created institutions to help in implementation, from regulatory bodies to semi-private investment corporations.

Morocco made its first major commitment to renewable energy in June 1992 when it signed the United Nations Framework Convention on Climate Change (UNFCCC) at the Earth Summit in Rio de Janeiro and later ratified the agreement in December 1995. But it was not until 2008, when King Mohammed VI launched the NES that the country began taking the necessary legal and institutional steps required to wean the country off energy imports and develop reliable renewable energy options. The strategy outlined a desire to decrease the country's dependence on imports, increase the accessibility of energy for rural and urban populations, stop the burgeoning cost increases, improve the efficiency in energy usage, and protect the environment.[37] According to Alaa Alhamwi et al., the King's NES "is one of the most ambitious and comprehensive renewable energy strategies in the Middle East and North Africa region."[38]

The next few years saw the government pass several laws in support of the NES that would reinforce and support the strategy. First, in January 2010, Law 57–09 created the Moroccan Agency for Solar Energy (MASEN), a joint-stock company that has become one of the most important bodies implementing the government's solar energy development strategy.[39] Then, Law 16–09 created the National Agency for the Promotion of Renewable

Energy and Energy Conservation (ADEREE), which was renamed as the Moroccan Agency for Energy Efficiency (AMEE) in 2016, and focuses on "reducing energy dependence, through the democratization of renewable energy (RE) and the promotion of energy efficiency (EE)."[40] Then a month later, in February 2010, Law 13–09 allowed business competition in the energy sector, renewable energy to access the electricity grid, the export of renewable energy, and construction on a pipeline for export.[41] And Law 99-12 created the National Charter for the Environment and Sustainable Development, which not only strengthened the legal measures to fight against pollution and climate change but also identified sustainable development and environmental responsibility as a core value.[42]

To reinforce the legal reforms, the government also created institutions like the Office National de l'Electricté et de l'Eau Potable (ONEE), a combination of the existing water and electricity departments, and the Institute for Research in Solar Energy and New Energies (IRESEN). The government also sought to partner with the private sector on long-term agreements that promote build-operate-transfer and IPP contracts.[43] ONEE, fully owned by the government, serves as the single buyer of power in the market and oversees the production, transport, and distribution of electricity; however, in 2010, the government also allowed for private transactions of power through IPPs. [44] IRESEN supports research and development of solar energy by funding and partnering on research projects.[45]

By 2016, when the world came together and signed the UNFCCC's climate agreement in Paris, the King was prepared to commit 42% of the country's installed electrical capacity to be produced by renewable sources by 2020 and 14% through hydropower, wind power, and solar power, respectively.[46] Morocco's Intended National Determined Contribution (INDC) also identified that in order to reach its goal of a 32% reduction in greenhouse gasses (GHGs) compared to business as usual (BAU) emissions by 2030, 50% of the mitigation efforts would occur from the energy sector.[47] Morocco also aspires to reduce energy consumption 12% by 2020 and 15% by 2030, with just under half of that savings coming from the energy sector.[48] The King's plan includes the government investing $8.3 billion on solar projects, $3.2 billion on wind energy projects, and $1.3 billion on hydropower plants, some of which are already in operation.[49]

Fossil fuels

While the NES committed to addressing the challenges of climate change, the King did not abandon the use of fossil fuels or the search to find new oil and gas reserves as a part of his energy independence strategy. But in order to attract exploration and development in a sector without proven reserves, the country has offered attractive incentives. This has resulted in investment in oil and gas exploration from 2010 to 2016 that surpassed $1.6 billion, 98% of which came from private partners, although the National Office of Hydrocarbons and Mines (ONHYM) has also invested its own efforts in assessing the feasibility of oil and gas extraction from shale, particularly in the Middle Atlas Mountains.[50] In 2016, two-thirds of the hydrocarbon licenses offered were offshore, covering nearly 123,000 square kilometers of Moroccan waters and included partnerships with Chariot Oil & Gas, Sound Energy, SDX Energy, and ENI.[51]

The most promising area has been the considerable gas reserves. According to a 2013 report by the US Energy Information Administration, Morocco has 20 trillion cubic feet (tcf) of recoverable shale oil and gas located mostly in the Tindouf basin, which covers southern Morocco and the Western Sahara, and the Tadla basin in central Morocco.[52] One energy company executive noted in 2013 that not only does "[Morocco] have all the conditions to find conventional gas," it also has the opportunity to find shale gas, which is "completely untapped."[53] And companies have been willing to continue to invest in so far unproven reserves because of the beneficial licensing permits the country has signed, like the 75% stake Sound Energy and its private partner Schlumberger control in an eastern Moroccan project.[54]

While these reserves would help reduce the country's energy dependence, that optimism has not yet led to significant increases in production and would hardly turn the county into a net exporter. As of 2017, Morocco was producing 3.1 billion cubic feet (bcf) in natural gas, but consuming 43 bcf.[55] In comparison, even Morocco's similarly energy-dependent neighbor, Tunisia, produces more natural gas (45 bcf) for domestic consumption.[56] However, a 2016 discovery of natural gas in Tendara, eastern Morocco, has raised some optimism. According to Sound Energy, the discovery holds 31 tcf of natural gas and will begin producing 60 million cubic feet per day over a ten-year period;[57] and with a pipeline approved to connect the gas to the existing Maghreb-Europe Gas Pipeline, the country could begin exporting modest amounts of natural gas.[58]

The pipeline represents an additional part of the strategy focused on processing and delivery projects, which hopes to strengthen the existing refining industry. At the beginning of 2018, Energy Minister Aziz Rabbah announced a tender for a $4.6 billion natural gas project to build a plant to process and provide the gas to industry.[59] While in May 2017, Morocco and Nigeria signed a cooperation agreement to build a gas pipeline between the two countries, which will eventually connect to the Maghreb-Europe Gas Pipeline.[60]

Historically, Morocco has relied on coal for much of its energy supply. In 2013, coal production provided over 50%[61] of the electricity and by 2030 coal is still expected to contribute over 20% of the installed capacity.[62] At one time, Morocco was mining much of its own coal, but since the late 1990s has relied on imports. The last major project to retain the coal mining industry came in 1985 at the Jerada coal mines. With World Bank support, the government intended to invest $27 million to modernize and expand the mines.[63] However, by 1991, it was clear the project was not economically feasible and the project was terminated after expending half of the World Bank loan. Not only did the project's actual cost skyrocket to $82.5 million, the global cost of coal plummeted and the mine was failing to meet production expectations.[64] The failure of the project and closing of the mine devastated the local region, costing over 9,000 jobs.[65]

As the mines closed permanently, thousands left looking for new work while others continued to mine illegally, often earning just $11 per day.[66] In 2017, protests erupted calling for "jobs and development" following the deaths of two miners in an abandoned pit. Protesters accused local officials of purchasing coal below market prices from those mining illegally, only to turn around and sell the coal for large profits.[67] In response, the King promised to address the region's concerns and install a coal power station near Jerada that would employ 500 locals.[68] The government also immediately closed 2,000 mineshafts and intended to close any other remaining shafts.[69] Although Morocco's domestic mining industry has receded, the country continues to invest in maintaining and expanding its coal-fired power production. In 2008, ONEE announced they had initiated a $2.7 billion IPP project to build a 1,300 MW coal power plant.[70]

Meanwhile, at the 2009 UNFCCC, Morocco indicated as part of its plan to reduce GHGs it would build two 1,000 MW nuclear reactors.[71] According to the International Atomic Energy Agency (IAEA), while Morocco has sought bids on developing local nuclear energy – benefited by its ability to extract uranium from the country's large phosphate reserves – the country has not yet completed a power plant for production.[72] In 2010, former French Prime Minister Francois Fillon signed a cooperation agreement with Morocco, although he insisted that it was not a commercial deal but a "framework accord that will help Morocco prepare entry into the field of nuclear energy."[73] That same year, US company General Atomics signed a deal to build a research reactor east of Rabat, and Atomstroyexport, a subsidiary of the Russian state-run nuclear energy company Rosatam, signed an agreement to build a nuclear power plant at Sidi Boulbra,[74] which the IAEA does not expect to begin commercial activities before 2030.[75]

Renewable energy

But King Mohammed VI's most ambitious energy project is in renewable energy, where the country is seeking to create 2,000 MW of power through hydroelectric, wind, and solar, respectively. The country maintains miles of windy coastline and regular sun-filled days throughout the country, making it a perfect candidate blessed with plentiful, naturally occurring, renewable resources. In 2001, Morocco hosted the seventh annual Conference of the Parties (COP 7), an annual meeting that seeks to address and further UNFCCC efforts.[76] And in November 2016, the King hosted COP 22,[77] which focused on implementation of the Paris agreement.[78] Signed by nearly every country in the world, the agreement is the largest breakthrough on climate change to date, where countries agreed to reduce their CO_2 emissions in an effort to keep temperatures below the two-degree threshold.[79]

Morocco's INDC, agreed upon in Paris, is a significant commitment to reduce its GHG emissions: 13% by 2030 without any international support and an additional 19% with international financial support.[80] To reach the overall 32% reduction by 2030, Morocco projects that it will need $45 billion, of which Morocco intends to contribute $10 billion.[81] In the INDC, the King declared his energy vision: "Make [Morocco's] territory and civilization more resilient to climate change while ensuring a rapid transition to a low-carbon economy."[82]

The King has been able to take advantage of increased international attention and investment in renewable energy. National, regional, and IFIs have supported renewable energy efforts, while private initiatives have also sought to influence the growth and development of renewable energy. Morocco signed the International Renewable Energy Agency statute in 2009 gaining international support for its transition to renewable energy, and has participated in the Solar Plan for the Mediterranean, a non-profit organization dedicated to helping companies and countries develop an "efficient collaborative action plan" for solar projects in the region.[83]

Lacking the funds to reach his goals, the King has looked to the international community for help through both loans and grants. As global concerns over climate change have grown, financial institutions have dedicated more funds to supporting climate change mitigation efforts. In 2008, the World Bank created the Climate Investment Funds (CIF) and separated the project into two trust funds, the Clean Technology Fund (CTF) and the Strategic Climate Fund (SCF). The CTF provides funds to developing countries for low-carbon technology projects that would reduce or avoid GHG emissions. The SCF seeks to help developing countries prepare for the effects of climate change and shift their development to become climate resilient. But the World Bank is not the only investor. Funders have partnered together, working through the CIF's multilateral funds focused on mitigation and adaptation and have pledged nearly $30 billion from 2003 to 2017.[84] Development financial institutions like the African Development Bank, national aid agencies like USAID, and the UN are among the numerous agencies and institutions implementing the funds.[85] And ultimately, most of the money has come from state support led by the United States, the United Kingdom, France, Germany, and Japan.[86]

As of November 2017, Morocco is the third largest recipient in the world for climate change funds with $784 million approved, below only Brazil and India, and has received over 60% of the financial investment for the Middle East and North Africa.[87] Egypt is the second largest recipient in the region with $397 million, just over half Morocco's pledged amount.[88] The CTF's largest investment is for the Noor CSP project at $238 million. The Kingdom has also been approved for $100 million in agricultural adaptation projects from the Green Climate Fund.[89] But the majority of the funds are dedicated toward mitigation projects (like the Noor plant), including $125 million for the One Wind Energy Plan and $6.2 million from the Global Environment Facility fund for energy efficiency projects in commercial and industrial spaces.[90]

The Mediterranean Solar Plan, launched by the Union for the Mediterranean, has helped Morocco implement renewable energy strategies and coordinate with European and Mediterranean countries. The Desertec initiative, which Morocco also joined, officially launched in 2009. According to the Desertec Foundation, "Emerging regions urgently need clean and reliable energy as the basis for prosperity, food and drinking water production," and, "at the same time, [Desertec] can accelerate the energy revolution of the rich world with energy imports from desert regions."[91] The plan envisions building renewable energy hubs across North Africa and exporting the energy to Europe, taking advantage of the regions undeveloped spaces and significantly higher number of days with no cloud cover. As the foundation notes, renewable energy can be transmitted up to 3,000 kilometers for consumption, within range of 90% of the world's population.[92] By 2014, Deutsche Bank, Siemens, Munich Reinsurance Company, and energy giants RWE and E.On had all invested in the initiative.[93] Besides the training and assistance, creating an interconnection with Europe through these initiatives, financial investments, and energy exports furthers one of the country's strategic goals of making itself indispensable to European Union (EU) countries.[94]

The King has also looked south in exporting both its electricity and electricity management expertise.[95] In December 2018, the government's official support for the G5 Sahel's Priority Investment Program, which includes electrification projects in Burkina Faso, Mali, Mauritania, Niger, and Chad, offers opportunities for Morocco to invest in energy projects in sub-Saharan Africa.[96]

Seeing the advantage of being an early leader to adopt renewable energy initiatives, the King has not only sought to gain energy independence and mitigate the effects of climate change but also use the investments to develop a domestic industry that can provide well-paid, highly skilled jobs to the Moroccan workforce. In developing the domestic energy industry, the challenge has been in acquiring capital and equipment, as well as the technical expertise and intellectual property that other countries and companies have developed over the past several decades.[97] Many companies, so far, have shown a willingness to partner with local Moroccan firms but have been unwilling to share the most vital technical details and the Moroccan labor force still lacks the technical experts to meet the industry's demands.[98]

Nevertheless, the King's strategic and comprehensive approach to addressing the country's energy needs has put it ahead of its peers in the region who also lack significant fossil fuel reserves and are facing similar effects caused by climate change. This gives Morocco an advantage for drawing further FDI and creating sustainable growth in its emerging energy sector.

Hydroelectric power

One-third of the King's renewable energy plan is to come from domestic hydroelectric power generation, the country's most developed of the three renewable energies. Morocco already has the infrastructure to build and produce hydropower plants. In fact, as of 2017, through 26 dams and micro-hydropower stations, Morocco had 1,770 MW of installed capacity, nearly at its 2020 goal of 2,000 MW. By 2030, the country plans to develop an additional 1,330 MW of hydropower.[99]

Hydroelectric projects are overseen by ONEE, which owns the transmission grid and offers contracts. ONEE has identified an additional 126 sites for future development of small and micro-hydropower plants (100–1,500 kilowatts), for a maximum potential of 300 MW.[100] Not all future development is scheduled to be small though; in 2018 Vinci SA, the world's largest construction company, signed a $341 million contract to build a hydroelectric power plant in southwest Morocco.[101] Ultimately, Morocco's hydropower is constrained due to its limited rivers and flowing water capable of power conversion; estimates put Morocco's maximum hydroelectric power capacity at 3,800 MW.[102] If the King achieves his 2030 goal, that would leave Morocco only 700 MW available for future hydropower development.

Renewable energy coming from hydroelectric power must also factor in the country's limited water resources needed for drinking and agriculture, which the King has done in the 2009 National Water Strategy by incorporating a dam's storage capacity along with its electricity generation capabilities.[103] As a result of Morocco's limited capacity for future development compared to wind and solar projects, as well as its well-developed current capacity, the Kingdom will rely on future hydropower development the least in order to reach its ambitious renewable energy goals of 52% of installed electricity power from renewable energy. Already in 2014, 22% of installed capacity came from hydroelectric power, which by 2020 is expected to decrease to 14% as a result of other renewable energy production.[104]

Wind power

The second most developed renewable energy industry is Morocco's wind power that in 2014 accounted for 10% of installed capacity with 780 MW, more than one-third of the way to its 2020 goal of 2,000 MW.[105] Morocco opened its first wind energy project in 2000 in Taroudant Province, south of Marrakesh, a farm with a maximum capacity of 50.4 MW. Since then, Morocco has developed onshore and offshore wind farm projects throughout the country, like the 300 MW farm in Tarfaya that opened in 2014, two projects in Tangier with a capacity of 450 MW that opened in 2016, and farms in the Atlas and Rif mountains. The Tarfaya project, one of the largest wind farms in Africa, cost $700 million, is comprised of 131 wind turbines, expected to reduce CO_2 emissions by 900,000 tons per year, and meets the energy requirements of hundreds of thousands of Moroccans.[106]

The country's capacity to develop wind energy, with its long shoreline and mountainous inland region, is exceptionally high. With an estimated 25,000 MW of potential power from wind energy, Morocco can become a global leader in production and development.[107] Helping the country build its wind power has been the declining global prices. In fact, in 2015, Morocco awarded a tender for a project for $.03 per kilowatt hour, a record low price globally for wind power and cheaper than coal.[108] The declining price of wind power is likely to help the country reach its 2030 goal of 4,200 MW. If it succeeds, then it would be a 438% increase from the country's 2014 installed capacity, but still far below its maximum capacity.

The Rif region, which has endured turmoil and conflict including renewed protests in 2017, has seen 276 MW of wind capacity developed in the region since 2000 and another 320 MW expected by 2020.[109] For a region still suffering from the closures of coal mines decades ago, these wind farms should offer job opportunities, reduced energy prices, and a cleaner local environment.

Meanwhile, at the end of 2017, Morocco exported the country's first "Made in Morocco" wind turbine, developed through a partnership at Siemens' Tangier factory. Ralph Sperrazza, the director of the Tangier plant, said the blades coming out of the plant are "among the largest single-piece composite parts in the world."[110] The King has invested heavily in the country's infrastructure, from its highways to ports, in order to ensure the feasibility of such a project. And the domestic industry has a strong potential of building off these successes having developed important knowledge over the past decade.[111] As IRENA has noted, "Moroccan companies have a great capability for innovation developing partnerships and technological cooperation with international companies, which would help them to produce blades locally for upcoming projects."[112]

Solar

The country's solar industry has drawn the most attention, from foreign investment to academic study, from its potential economic impact to its effect on climate change. And the King's efforts in solar are the most ambitious part of his renewable energy strategy. Morocco's most ambitious project to date is the Noor Power Station, operational as of February 2016, that when fully completed will provide electricity to over one million Moroccans, cover an area as large as 3,000 hectares, and save an estimated 760,000 tons in carbon emissions per year.[113] Already the plant is the world's largest CSP plant with 537,000 mirrors,[114] supplying 360,000 people with electricity, and avoiding 217,000 tons of GHGs per year.[115] Financing the project cost an estimated $2.7 billion, with initial money supplied by the World Bank's International Bank for Reconstruction and Development ($400 million) and CTF ($238 million), in addition to various multilateral and national institutions like the African Development

Bank ($135 million), European Investment Bank ($473 million), and the German development bank KfW ($884 million).[116]

CSP technology costs more than photovoltaic (PV) panels and needs water for the plant's mirrors, a particular vulnerability for Morocco which lacks prevalent water resources.[117] But the benefit of CSP is its ability to better store energy during cloudy days and evenings when the plant is unable to utilize the sun's energy. Because of the benefits, Morocco has committed to expanding CSP beyond the Noor Ouarzazate project, to four other CSP complexes by 2020 including two plants Foum Al Oued and Sebkhat Tha in southern Morocco; Boujdour in Western Sahara; and Aïn Béni Mathar in northern Morocco. By completing these projects, the country will reach its goal of 2,000 MW of installed capacity from solar energy by 2020, over one-quarter (560 MW) coming from the Noor plant.[118]

According to the International Renewable Energy Agency, Morocco's solar PV industry offers the highest potential for domestic growth in the medium term.[119] The country already has a nascent industry with the capability to produce several necessary components for PV plants but has required cooperation with foreign companies for some manufacturing.[120] While PV panels are cheaper to develop, CSP has received more interest by foreign investors.[121] For Morocco's projects, most equipment has been manufactured abroad and then imported and installed in country, typically coming from the United States, France, Spain, or Germany, but limiting the industry's growth.[122]

Not all of the solar projects are large plants though. The National Program on Solar Pumps, launched in 2013, is an example of an intergovernmental and private sector project that wants to provide solar-powered water pumps for small- and medium-sized farmers.[123] A part of the Green Morocco Plan, a strategy for sustainable agriculture, the solar-powered water pumps project is an example of the King understanding the interconnectedness of the energy sector with that of other industries like agriculture.

Interest in developing solar energy from the King and international investors is in part a recognition that Morocco's solar energy capacity is extensive with annual sunshine ranging from 2,700 hours per year in the north to 3,500 hours in the south.[124] But the King wants to do more than just build plants across the country. He hopes to build a domestic solar industry. Three major challenges – all interconnected – have hindered the country's ability to develop a more substantial domestic industry. First, the major manufacturing stages, like glass production and automation for mounting structures, are capital intensive.[125] While some international support has focused on helping domestic industries, the barrier to entry remains significant. Morocco has the capability to manufacture and deliver several stages of production including construction, cables, and piping, but none of the significant value-added stages. Second, the country still lacks the advanced technological knowhow required to develop a CSP plant.[126] As it stands

Morocco's manufacturing base relies on international companies to make their capabilities profitable, particularly given the limited market in the region. Finally, the country lacks the number of highly skilled professionals needed to effectively build a competitive industry.[127] Despite the significant business-related challenges that exist, according to the research of Ramon Mahia et al., it was government officials' "distorting presence" and the lack of a clear fiscal and legislative framework that was the greatest barrier to developing a domestic industry.[128]

The King hopes the efforts at becoming a leader in renewable energy will not only address Morocco's climate and dependency concerns but also make the country competitive in the international renewable energy market. Already Morocco's Nareva Holding, a subsidiary of the National Investment Company (SNI), has signed an agreement with Engie, a low-carbon energy company, to expand its partnership from the Tarfaya wind farm project to other parts of North and West Africa.[129] And the World Bank with Ithmar Capital, a Moroccan sovereign investment fund, signed a memorandum of understanding to create the Green Growth Infrastructure Facility for Africa (GGIF Africa), the first ever pan-African fund dedicated to green investment on the continent.[130] If Morocco is successful, these large-scale projects could prove fruitful domestically and internationally.

However, much of the successful implementation of the King's ambitious renewable energy goals rests on several mega-wind and solar power projects. Dorothea Richewski, the director of the Heinrich Boll Foundation in Rabat, is concerned that Morocco is too reliant on international financial support and projects like Noor Ouarzazate will see "Morocco's dependency on fossil fuels be replaced by a financial dependency."[131] Prices for renewable energy projects have decreased, but it is still unclear if these mega-projects can gain economic sustainability justifying their initial investment.

Most analysts have rightly commended the country for its commitment to improving its energy sector and incorporating renewable energy strategies. However, Karen Eugenie Rignall's research has documented how the government's acquisition of land, particularly in areas with a long history of marginalization, has taken advantage of "open" tribal land.[132] For example, while it was reported that all of the local residents near the Noor plant in Ouarzazate would be compensated,[133] Rignall indicates that the money was actually placed in an account within the Ministry of Interior held in the Ait Oukrour tribes name, but no tribal members had access.[134] Instead, the funds were used to finance development projects in the region with minimal local input.[135] Rignall suggests that local activists "found that their space for political maneuver was circumscribed not only by the 'progressive' discourses of renewable energy but also by entrenched modes of governmentality that reduced populations to objects of development."[136]

At the same time, not only was the project going to help the country address its energy dependence and GHG emissions, but by the end of the Noor plant's first year in operation, MASEN was reporting that it had exceeded expectations and was already improving service and eliminating blackouts in the local community.[137]

The King has invested heavily in creating an energy sector that is both built for the challenges of the 21st century and capable of fueling growth. Unlike in the 1990s, Morocco is better positioned to take advantage of the new technologies spurring growth and development around the world. It has continued to use and invest in fossil fuels, but its leapfrog strategy to embrace renewable energy has allowed it to become a global renewable energy leader and create a nascent industry of its own. The King showed the initiative and emphasized the importance of creating the legal and institutional frameworks necessary to develop the sector. However, the country still needs to continue to make progress by providing better training for the industry's jobs, ensuring land acquisition and industry regulation is done equitably, and following through on its renewable energy commitments. The King's approach has reduced the country's energy dependency, taken advantage of its natural resources, and positioned itself as a leader in one of the emerging global industries. It has also been an important step in a larger development strategy that has positioned the country to effectively grow and expand despite its lack of fossil fuels.

Notes

1 Energy Imports, Net (% of Energy Use). (n.d.). *The World Bank*. Retrieved August 6, 2018, from https://data.worldbank.org/indicator/EG.IMP.CONS. ZS?locations=MA.
2 Andiva, Y. (2018, October 19). Morocco to Invest US $40bn in Energy Sector. *Construction Review Online*. Retrieved from https://constructionreviewonline. com/2018/10/morocco-to-invest-us-40bn-in-the-energy-sector/.
3 Verme, P., El-Massnaoui, K., & Araar, A. (2014, February). *Economic Premise: Reforming Subsidies in Morocco* (Rep. No. 134). Retrieved from http://documents. worldbank.org/curated/en/621831468053942440/pdf/845160BRI00Box 382123B00PUBLIC00EP134.pdf (p. 1).
4 Ibid. World Bank. (1994, July). *Morocco: Repowering of Power Plant*, p. 2.
5 World Bank. (1994, July). *Morocco: Repowering of Power Plant* (Rep.). Retrieved   http://documents.worldbank.org/curated/en/703181468757834997/pdf/ multi0page.pdf (p. 1).
6 Ibid., p. 4.
7 Ibid., p. 1.
8 Verme, P., El-Massnaoui, K., & Araar, A. (2014, February). *Economic Premise: Reforming Subsidies in Morocco*, p. 1.
9 IMF Survey: Costly Mideast Subsidies Need Better Targeting. (2012, May 14). *International Monetary Fund*. Retrieved from https://www.imf.org/en/News/ Articles/2015/09/28/04/53/socar051412b.
10 Houzir, M., Mokass, M., & Schalatek, L. (2016, November 2). *Climate Governance and the Role of Climate Finance in Morocco* (Rep.). Retrieved from https:// us.boell.org/sites/default/files/morocco_study_climate_governance_final_ english_nov.2.pdf (p. 64).

11 Hamane, T. (2016). *A Snapshot of Morocco's Power Sector* (Rep.). Retrieved April 9, 2018, from Africa Energy Yearbook. Retrieved from: http://www. energynet.co.uk/webfm_send/2025 (p. 41).

12 Fakir, I. (2016, December 15). Will 'Lip Service' Reforms End Up Changing Morocco's Politics? *World Politics Review.* Retrieved from https://www. worldpoliticsreview.com/articles/20723/will-lip-service-reforms-end-up-changing-moroccos-politics.

13 IMF Survey: Morocco Taps $6.2 Billion Precautionary Loan. (2012, August 3). *International Monetary Fund.* Retrieved from https://www.imf.org/en/News/ Articles/2015/09/28/04/53/socar080312b.

14 *Morocco: Ex Post Evaluation of Exceptional Access under the 2012 Precautionary and Liquidity Line Arrangement* (Rep.). (2015, August 6). Retrieved from https://www.imf.org/en/Publications/CR/Issues/2016/12/31/Morocco-Ex-Post-Evaluation-of-Exceptional-Access-Under-the-2012-Precautionary-and-Liquidity-43188.

15 Jebari, I. (2016, September 13). Populist Limits to Subsidy Reforms in Morocco. *Carnegie Endowment for International Peace.* Retrieved from https:// carnegieendowment.org/sada/?fa=64557.

16 Ibid.

17 Houzir, M., Mokass, M., & Schalatek, L. (2016, November 2). *Climate Governance and the Role of Climate Finance in Morocco*, p. 58.

18 *The World Factbook: Morocco.* (2018, February 1). Retrieved from https://www. cia.gov/library/publications/the-world-factbook/geos/mo.html.

19 Ibid.

20 Houzir, M., Mokass, M., & Schalatek, L. (2016, November 2). *Climate Governance and the Role of Climate Finance in Morocco*, p. 24.

21 Ibid., p. 16.

22 IPCC. (2007). *Climate Change 2007: Synthesis Report. Contribution of Working Groups I, II and III to the Fourth Assessment Report of the Intergovernmental Panel on Climate Change* [Core Writing Team, R. K Pachauri and A. Reisinger (eds.)]. IPCC, Geneva, Switzerland, p. 104.

23 *The Green Economy in Morocco: A Strategic Goal Involving Partnerships Dynamics and Intensified Coordination of Policies and Initiatives* (Rep.). (n.d.). Retrieved from https://www.uneca.org/sites/default/files/uploaded-documents/ SROs/NA/AHEGM-ISDGE/egm_ge-_morocco.pdf (p. 4).

24 *The World Factbook: Morocco.* (2018, February 1).

25 Houzir, M., Mokass, M., & Schalatek, L. (2016, November 2). *Climate Governance and the Role of Climate Finance in Morocco*, p. 11.

26 Ibid., p. 13.

27 Burck, J., Hagen, U., Marten, F., Höhne, N., & Bals, C. (2019). *Climate Change Performance Index: Results 2019* (Rep.). Retrieved from Germanwatch and Climate Action Network Europe: https://germanwatch.org/sites/germanwatch. org/files/CCPI2019_Results_WEB.pdf (p. 7).

28 Ibid. Burck, J., Hagen, U., Marten, F., & Bals, C. (2015). *Climate Change Performance Index: Results 2015* (Rep). Retrieved from Germanwatch and Climate Action Network Europe https://germanwatch.org/sites/germanwatch.org/files/ publication/10407.pdf (p. 5).

29 Burck, J., Hagen, U., Marten, F., Höhne, N., & Bals, C. (2019). *Climate Change Performance Index: Results 2019*, p. 16.

30 *Renewable energy country attractiveness index: From black gold to green power* (Rep. No. 51). (2018, May). Retrieved from Ernst and Young https://www. qualenergia.it/wp-content/uploads/2018/05/recai-51-may-2018.pdf (p. 11).

31 Bazza, T. (2018, October 2). Energy Minister: Morocco to Invest $30 Billion in Renewable Energy by 2030. *Morocco World News.* Retrieved from https://www.

moroccoworldnews.com/2018/10/254477/energy-minister-morocco-to-invest-30-billion-in-renewable-energy-by-2030/.
32 Mohamed, S. E., & Sidiropoulos, M. G. (2010). Another Look at the Determinants of Foreign Direct Investment in MENA Countries: An Empirical. *Journal of Economic Development*, 35(2), 75–95. Retrieved from https://search-proquest-com.proxy1.library.jhu.edu/docview/737530324?accountid=11752 (p. 88).
33 Mahia, R., Arce, R. D., & Medina, E. (2014). Assessing the Future of a CSP Industry in Morocco. *Energy Policy*, 69, 586–597. doi:10.1016/j.enpol.2014.02.024 (p. 587).
34 Fritzsche, K., Zejli, D., & Tänzler, D. (2011). The Relevance of Global Energy Governance for Arab Countries: The Case of Morocco. *Energy Policy*, 39(8), 4497–4506. doi:10.1016/j.enpol.2010.11.042 (p. 4498).
35 Andiva, Y. (2018, October 19). Morocco to Invest US $40bn in Energy Sector.
36 Hamane, T. (2016). *A Snapshot of Morocco's Power Sector*, p. 39.
37 Kousksou, T., Allouhi, A., Belattar, M., Jamil, A., Rhafiki, T. E., Arid, A., & Zeraouli, Y. (2015). Renewable Energy Potential and National Policy Directions for Sustainable Development in Morocco. *Renewable and Sustainable Energy Reviews*, 46–57. doi:10.1016/j.rser.2015.02.056 (p. 49).
38 Alhamwi, A., Kleinhans, D., Weitemeyer, S., & Vogt, T. (2015). Moroccan National Energy Strategy Reviewed from a Meteorological Perspective. *Energy Strategy Reviews*, 6, 39–47. doi:10.1016/j.esr.2015.02.002 (p. 39).
39 Kousksou, T., Allouhi, A., Belattar, M., Jamil, A., Rhafiki, T. E., Arid, A., & Zeraouli, Y. (2015), p. 49.
40 Our Charter. (n.d.). Retrieved October 2, 2018, from http://www.amee.ma/index.php?option=com_content&view=article&id=114&Itemid=229&lang=en.
41 Kousksou, T., Allouhi, A., Belattar, M., Jamil, A., Rhafiki, T. E., Arid, A., & Zeraouli, Y. (2015), p. 49.
42 Houzir, M., Mokass, M., & Schalatek, L. (2016, November 2). *Climate Governance and the Role of Climate Finance in Morocco*, p. 30.
43 Kousksou, T., Allouhi, A., Belattar, M., Jamil, A., Rhafiki, T. E., Arid, A., & Zeraouli, Y. (2015), p. 49.
44 Hamane, T. (2016). *A Snapshot of Morocco's Power Sector*, p. 39.
45 IRESEN. (n.d.). Description. Retrieved from http://www.iresen.org/institute/?lang=en.
46 *Morocco: Intended Nationally Determined Contribution (INDC) Under the UNFCCC* (Rep.). (2015, June 5). Retrieved from https://www4.unfccc.int/sites/submissions/INDC/Published Documents/Morocco/1/Morocco%20INDC%20submitted%20to%20UNFCCC%20-%205%20june%202015.pdf.
47 Ibid.
48 Ibid.
49 Houzir, M., Mokass, M., & Schalatek, L. (2016, November 2). *Climate Governance and the Role of Climate Finance in Morocco*, p. 52.
50 Asraoui, S. (2017, September 29). Morocco's Sedimentary Basins Not Sufficiently Explored: ONHYM. *Morocco World News*. Retrieved from https://www.moroccoworldnews.com/2017/09/229660/moroccos-sedimentary-basins-not-sufficiently-explored-onhym/.
51 *Annual Report 2017* (Rep.). (n.d.). Retrieved from National Office of Hydrocarbons and Mines (ONHYM) http://www.onhym.com/pdf/Publications/RAPPORT_en_2017.pdf (pp. 12, 16).
52 Kan, C. (2014). Morocco's Gas Rush. *Middle East*, (451), 40. Retrieved from http://search.ebscohost.com.proxy1.library.jhu.edu/login.aspx?direct=true&db=f5h&AN=94716529&site=ehost-live&scope=site.
53 Ibid.
54 Lahsini, C. (2017, August 1). Sound Energy Gets Green Light to Build Gas Export Pipeline in Eastern Morocco. *Morocco World News*. Retrieved from https://

www.moroccoworldnews.com/2017/08/225076/sound-energy-build-gas-export-pipeline-eastern-morocco/.

55 The World Factbook: Morocco. (2018, February 1).
56 The World Factbook: Tunisia. (2018, February 1). Retrieved from https://www.cia.gov/library/publications/the-world-factbook/geos/ts.html.
57 Fihri, O. F. (2018, October 15). Morocco to Diversify Its Energy Sources with Natural Gas. *Morocco World News*. Retrieved from https://www.moroccoworld news.com/2018/10/255352/morocco-energy-lng-natural-gas/.
58 Sound Energy Moves to Develop Tendrara Concession. (2018, June 10). *Pipeline Oil and Gas Magazine*. Retrieved from https://www.pipelineoilandgasnews.com/regionalinternational-news/regional-news/2018/june/sound-energy-moves-to-develop-tendrara-concession/.
59 Habboush, M. (2018, January 15). Morocco to Tender for $4.6-Billion Natural Gas Project. *World Oil*. Retrieved from https://www.worldoil.com/news/2018/1/15/morocco-to-tender-for-46-billion-natural-gas-project.
60 *Annual Report 2017*, p. 15.
61 Kousksou, T., Allouhi, A., Belattar, M., Jamil, A., Rhafiki, T. E., Arid, A., & Zeraouli, Y. (2015). p. 48.
62 Hamane, T. (2016). *A Snapshot of Morocco's Power Sector*, p. 40.
63 World Bank. (1993, June 24). *Project Completion Report: Morocco-Jerada Coal Mine Modernization and Expansion Project* (Rep.). Retrieved from http://documents.worldbank.org/curated/en/366101468324565888/pdf/multi-page.pdf (p. i).
64 Ibid., p. ii.
65 Morocco closes 2 000 mine shafts after string of deaths. (2019, January 10). *Agence France-Presse*. Retrieved from https://www.news24.com/Africa/News/morocco-closes-2-000-mine-shafts-after-string-of-deaths-20190110.
66 COAL: Morocco. (2018), *Africa Research Bulletin Economics*, 54, 21979C–21980A. doi:10.1111/j.1467-6346.2018.08126.x.
67 Ibid
68 Ibid.
69 Morocco closes 2 000 mine shafts after string of deaths. (2019, January 10).
70 *2008 Minerals Yearbook: Morocco and Western Sahara* (Rep.). (2010, September). Retrieved from https://minerals.usgs.gov/minerals/pubs/country/2008/myb3-2008-mo-wi.pdf (p. 30.3)
71 Bahgat, G. (2013). Morocco Energy Outlook: Opportunities and Challenges. *The Journal of North African Studies*, 18(2), 291–304. doi:10.1080/13629387.2012.726089 (p. 295).
72 Morocco: Country Energy Overview. (2018). Retrieved February 8, 2019, from https://cnpp.iaea.org/countryprofiles/Morocco/Morocco.htm.
73 Bahgat, G. (2013). Morocco Energy Outlook: Opportunities and Challenges, p. 294.
74 Ibid.
75 Morocco: Country Energy Overview. (2018).
76 COP 7. (2001, October/November). Retrieved from https://unfccc.int/process/conferences/past-conferences/marrakech-climate-change-conference-october-2001/cop-7.
77 COP 22. (2016, October/November). Retrieved from https://unfccc.int/process-and-meetings/conferences/past-conferences/marrakech-climate-change-conference-november-2016/cop-22.
78 The Paris Agreement. (2018, October 22). Retrieved from https://unfccc.int/process-and-meetings/the-paris-agreement/the-paris-agreement.
79 Ibid.
80 *Morocco: Intended Nationally Determined Contribution (INDC) Under the UNFCCC*.

81 Ibid.
82 Ibid.
83 Mediterranean Solar Plan. (2016). PREFACE – THE CONSORTIUM. Retrieved from https://www.plansolairemediterraneen.org/preface-the-consortium/.
84 Data Dashboard. (2019, February). Retrieved from https://climatefundsupdate. org/data-dashboard/#1541245664232-8e27b692-05c8.
85 Global Climate Finance Architecture. (n.d.). Retrieved from https://climatefunds update.org/about-climate-finance/global-climate-finance-architecture/.
86 Data Dashboard. (2019, February). Retrieved from https://climatefundsupdate. org/data-dashboard/#1541245664327-538690dc-b9a8.
87 Data Dashboard. (2019, February). Retrieved from https://climatefundsupdate. org/data-dashboard/#1541245745457-d3cda887-f010.
88 Ibid.
89 Ibid.
90 Ibid.
91 Desertec. (n.d.). Retrieved from http://www.desertec.org/.
92 The Desertec Concept. (n.d.). Retrieved from http://www.desertec.org/the-concept.
93 Kousksou, T., Allouhi, A., Belattar, M., Jamil, A., Rhafiki, T. E., Arid, A., & Zeraouli, Y. (2015), p. 55.
94 Rignall, K. E. (2015). Solar Power, State Power, and the Politics of Energy Transition in Pre-Saharan Morocco. *Environment and Planning A: Economy and Space*, 48(3), 540–557. doi:10.1177/0308518x15619176 (p. 544).
95 Fakir, I. (2019, January 23). Morocco Looks South. *Carnegie Endowment for International Peace*. Retrieved from https://carnegie-mec.org/diwan/78189.
96 G5 Sahel Permanent Secretariat. (2018, October). *Priority Investment Program (PIP/G5 Sahel) First Phase 2019–2021* (Rep.). Retrieved from https://www. g5sahel.org/images/DOCPIP/PIP_G5S_EN__VF.pdf (p. 5).
97 Fritzsche, K., Zejli, D., & Tänzler, D. (2011). The Relevance of Global Energy Governance for Arab Countries: The Case of Morocco. *Energy Policy*, p. 4501.
98 Ibid.
99 Redouane, A., Masaki, M., Meijer, M., & Essakkati, H. (2018). *Business Opportunities Report for Morocco's Renewable Energy Sector* (Rep.). Netherlands Enterprise Agency. Retrieved from https://www.rijksoverheid.nl/binaries/ rijksoverheid/documenten/rapporten/2018/06/01/business-opportunities-report-for-morocco's-renewable-energy-sector/business-opportunities-report-for-morocco's-renewable-energy-sector.pdf (p. 47).
100 Redouane, A., Masaki, M., Meijer, M., & Essakkati, H. (2018). *Business Opportunities Report for Morocco's Renewable Energy Sector*, p. 60.
101 Allen, N. (2018, January 9). Vinci Signs EUR284 Million Hydroelectric Contract in Morocco. *Fox Business*. Retrieved from https://www.foxbusiness.com/ features/vinci-signs-eur284-million-hydroelectric-contract-in-morocco.
102 Redouane, A., Masaki, M., Meijer, M., & Essakkati, H. (2018). *Business Opportunities Report for Morocco's Renewable Energy Sector*, p. 60.
103 Houzir, M., Mokass, M., & Schalatek, L. (2016, November 2). *Climate Governance and the Role of Climate Finance in Morocco*, pp. 22–23.
104 Alhamwi, A., Kleinhans, D., Weitemeyer, S., & Vogt, T. (2015). *Moroccan National Energy Strategy Reviewed from a Meteorological Perspective*, p. 40.
105 Ibid.
106 Redouane, A., Masaki, M., Meijer, M., & Essakkati, H. (2018). *Business Opportunities Report for Morocco's Renewable Energy Sector*, p. 59.
107 Ibid., p. 60.
108 Ibid., p. 59.

109 Ibid., pp. 51–52.
110 First 'Made in Morocco' Wind Turbine Leaves Tanger Med Port. (2017, December 13). *Morocco World News.* Retrieved from https://www.moroccoworldnews. com/2017/12/236258/made-morocco-wind-turbine-tanger-med-port-siemens-gamesa/.
111 *Evaluating Renewable Energy Manufacturing Potential in the Mediterranean Partner Countries* (Rep.). (2015). International Renewable Energy Agency. Retrieved from https://www.eib.org/attachments/femip_study_evaluating_renewable_ energy_manufacturing_potential_en.pdf (p. 112).
112 Ibid., p. 11.
113 Parke, P., & Giles, C. (2018, May 17). Morocco's Megawatt Solar Plant Powers Up. *CNN.* Retrieved from https://www.cnn.com/2016/02/08/africa/ouarzazate-morocco-solar-plant/index.html.
114 Houzir, M., Mokass, M., & Schalatek, L. (2016, November 2). *Climate Governance and the Role of Climate Finance in Morocco*, p. 69.
115 MA- Noor Ouarzazate Concentrated Solar Power Project. (n.d.). Retrieved February 21, 2019, from http://projects.worldbank.org/P131256/?lang=en&tab= results.
116 Ibid.
117 Moroccan Green Energy Receives Key AfDB Backing. (2013). *New African*, (528), 90. Retrieved from http://search.ebscohost.com.proxy1.library. jhu.edu/login.aspx?direct=true&db=f5h&AN=87732019&site=ehost-live& scope=site.
118 Houzir, M., Mokass, M., & Schalatek, L. (2016, November 2). *Climate Governance and the Role of Climate Finance in Morocco*, p. 69.
119 *Evaluating Renewable Energy Manufacturing Potential in the Mediterranean Partner Countries* (Rep.). (2015). p. 11.
120 Ibid.
121 Moroccan Green Energy Receives Key AfDB Backing. (2013).
122 Mahia, R., Arce, R. D., & Medina, E. (2014). Assessing the Future of a CSP Industry in Morocco, p. 587.
123 Plan Maroc Vert: Agriculture in a Changing Climate. (2014, January 24). Retrieved from http://www.worldbank.org/en/news/video/2014/01/24/supporting-small-farmers-in-morocco.
124 Kousksou, T., Allouhi, A., Belattar, M., Jamil, A., Rhafiki, T. E., Arid, A., & Zeraouli, Y. (2015), p. 52.
125 Mahia, R., Arce, R. D., & Medina, E. (2014). Assessing the future of a CSP industry in Morocco. p. 589.
126 Ibid., p. 593.
127 Ibid., p. 589.
128 Ibid.
129 Engie Signs Deal with Morocco's Nareva to Expand in Africa. (2016, June 24). *Reuters.* Retrieved from https://af.reuters.com/article/cameroonNews/ idAFL8N19G6LZ.
130 Morocco, World Bank to Create Green Growth Infrastructure Facility for Africa. (2016, November 17). *Morocco World News.* Retrieved from https://www.moroccoworldnews.com/2016/11/201576/morocco-world-bank-create-green-growth-infrastructure-facility-africa/.
131 Bruneau, C. (2016, November 15). Morocco Takes Lead in Climate Change Fight, but at What Cost? *Al-Monitor.* Retrieved from https://www.al-monitor. com/pulse/originals/2016/11/morocco-green-energy-sector-western-sahara. html#ixzz5iUh4Vtqf.
132 Rignall, K. E. (2015). Solar Power, State Power, and the Politics of Energy Transition in Pre-Saharan Morocco. p. 542.

133 *Non Technical Summary: Ouarzazate Solar Power Complex – SESIA* (Rep.). (2012, December). Retrieved from https://www.eib.org/attachments/pipeline/ 20100242_nts_en.pdf (p. xii).
134 Ibid. Rignall, K. E. (2015). p. 550.
135 Ibid.
136 Ibid., p. 551.
137 CSP Puts End to Morocco Electricity Blackouts. (2018, January 11). *SolarPaces.* Retrieved from http://www.solarpaces.org/csp-puts-end-morocco-electricity-blackouts/.

6 One Morocco for the haves, one for the have-nots

Morocco has successfully implemented many of its national strategies, like establishing the country as a global trading hub and resurrecting a once dying automotive industry. However, despite the numerous initiatives implemented, the country has not progressed nearly as far as it would have hoped for in the past 20 years since King Mohammed VI ascended the throne. In 1999, the United Nations' (UN) Human Development Index (HDI) ranked Morocco 126. In 2018, two decades later, Morocco ranked 123, only above Yemen in the MENA region.[1] And from 2010 to 2017, the Atlas method of gross national income (GNI) per capita, which accounts for inflation, actually decreased from $2,930 to $2,860.[2]

Morocco has embraced many of the neoliberal demands pressed upon it by the Bretton Woods Institutions (BWI) and the western countries that lead those institutions. Yet, many of the steps the country has taken have not resulted in the development that the BWIs and the Kingdom would have hoped for, particularly for the average Moroccan. Unemployment, poverty, and inequality remain significant challenges that have continued to plague the country and increasingly Moroccans feel that there are two economies, one for the well-connected and the other for those being left behind. They have seen multinational corporations come in and thrive, but little trickle down to them, and those with access manipulate the system with impunity. Unsurprisingly, the frustrations that emerged in 2011 – and led to a new constitution – have reemerged since 2016 and resulted in regular protests and other civic action throughout the country.

One area that has drawn the ire of citizens around the world is the corruption among elites, which has created the feeling of a rigged system. In fact, more than 10% of the world's countries "have experienced corruption-driven" leadership change in just four years, from 2014 to 2018.[3] Protests around the world have brought down corrupt regimes and also defeated well-established incumbents in elections. A growing global impatience has developed for governments, democratic, or authoritarian, that steal for power or wealth and violate the society's social contract. As Thomas Carothers and Christopher Carothers note, "Corruption has become a remarkably powerful – arguably the most powerful – issue driving political change in the world today."[4]

For the Kingdom, the challenge has been to expand the economic opportunities for all Moroccans. As entrepreneur Fritz-Earle Mc Lymont incisively notes, corporations, other large enterprises, and the well-connected are often able to simply write off corruption costs (if not gain financially from a deal), but small companies and emerging entrepreneurs are not able to compete with these additional costs of doing business.[5] Similarly, Rachid Aourraz, a founder of the Moroccan Institute for Policy Analysis, notes that despite the country's economic liberalization efforts, it has "failed to curtail the dominance of [a] rent economy," making it difficult for startups, entrepreneurs, and small- and medium-sized enterprises (SME) to succeed.[6] These obstacles have hindered the country's economic development, particularly for the majority of Moroccans who lack the right connections.

Like any country, Morocco has limited government resources. And when a country misuses funds, it creates inefficiencies and waste in the system. This results in increased inequality, the deterioration of the rule of law and good governance, and the weakening of society's trust in government institutions. In addition, when bribes are necessary to obtain the appropriate licenses, the cost of doing business increases while the competitiveness of the business decreases. When government contracts, loans, and grants are misused to preserve access, patronage, and rents, this not only scares off foreign direct investment but also crowds out private competition, particularly from local SMEs which are vital to improve productivity, enhance technological capabilities, and reduce costs. All of which stunts economic growth and the betterment of society.

This challenge was exemplified when Uber, after three years of legal and physical difficulties including harassment from the "Taxi Hawks," suspended its service in Morocco. Twelve thousand drivers, who if they worked full time could earn twice as much as the minimum wage (2,750 dirhams), lost their jobs.[7] While legitimate concerns existed from taxi drivers over increased competition, as Aourraz notes, the distribution of taxi licenses was "based less on objective criteria, like competence or merit, as it was on the criteria of loyalty to the Makhzen."[8] What this example best demonstrates is that the existing roadblocks to more thorough development remain despite the King's modernization efforts. In this case, consumers and tourists lose a more cost-efficient way to navigate Moroccan cities and the country loses a chance to integrate modern technologies into its socioeconomic development.[9]

In Morocco, there have long been whispers and concerns over corruption. In 2007, during several research trips, Guilain Denoeux commonly heard Moroccans complain that Morocco "has been spared weapons of mass destruction, but...is being destroyed by weapons of mass corruption."[10] And according to Sarah Chayes, frustration among some of the February 20th

Movement focused not just on economic opportunity but on the corruption among elites. In interviews on the streets of Rabat, she notes that Moroccans were telling her

> what was pushing people over the edge wasn't just poverty or misfortune in general—it was poverty in combination with acute injustice: the visible, daily contrast between ordinary people's privations and the ostentatious display of lavish wealth corruptly siphoned off by ruling cliques from what was broadly understood to be public resources.[11]

Quantitative studies support what scholars have been reporting from the field. In 2016, nearly 20% of Moroccans cited corruption as their top concern, the second highest concern among Moroccans only behind the two-thirds worried about the economy.[12] Meanwhile, three-quarters of all Moroccans suggested corruption was a large or moderate problem.[13] In 2017, Transparency International's (TI) annual Corruptions Perceptions Index ranked Morocco 81 out of 180 countries surveyed, close to where they have scored for over a decade.[14] According to TI, in 2017, 48% of Moroccans said they had paid a bribe in the last 12 months when accessing public services, compared to 14% for Algerians, 9% for Tunisians, and 18% for Turks, respectively.[15]

TI classifies corruption as "grand, petty and political, depending on the amounts of money lost and the sector where it occurs," and defines them as follows:

> Grand corruption consists of acts committed at a high level of government that distort policies or the central functioning of the state, enabling leaders to benefit at the expense of the public good. Petty corruption refers to everyday abuse of entrusted power by low- and mid-level public officials in their interactions with ordinary citizens, who often are trying to access basic goods or services in places like hospitals, schools, police departments and other agencies. Political corruption is a manipulation of policies, institutions and rules of procedure in the allocation of resources and financing by political decision makers, who abuse their position to sustain their power, status and wealth.[16]

The King has not been a passive observer ignoring the issue, but has tried to root out various types of corruption. From the time Mohammed VI ascended the throne in 1999, he took several steps to address the worst abuses of his father. This led many to suggest that he was going to be the "King of the Poor." And one of those steps was to begin more thoroughly addressing corruption. In fact, he has helped usher in an extensive legal and regulatory regime that, if implemented, has the authority to effectively combat corruption.

His first step came shortly after the 2003 Casablanca bombings, still one of the deadliest terror attacks to occur within the country, when the government issued a new anti-terrorism law that would allow officials to better combat money laundering.[17] Then in December 2003, Morocco signed the United Nations Convention Against Corruption (UNCAC) and ratified it in 2007, agreeing to take responsive as well as proactive measures to reduce corruption.[18] But the first positive step actually came a year before Mohammed VI became king, when King Hassan II granted legal status to Transparency Maroc, TI's Morocco chapter, after several years of the organization working without legal status.[19] This was an important step in supporting civil society's role in government oversight.

Building on these early steps, King Mohammed VI's government went further and in 2007 passed comprehensive anti-money laundering legislation as well as asset and income disclosure legislation for civil servants.[20] The government also took steps to institutionalize anti-corruption with the creation of the Central Agency for the Prevention of Corruption (ACPC) that was charged with

> collecting and disseminating information relating to corruption; helping to coordinate policies along several dimensions at both the central and sub-national levels; educating and sensitizing the public to corruption related issues; and serving as the focal point for monitoring progress in implementing the United Nations Convention against Corruption.[21]

Helping solidify its anti-corruption efforts, Morocco's penal code prohibited corruption-related offenses like embezzlement, collusion, conflicts of interest, bribery, and abuse of public office for private gain or influence; and these legal and institutional improvements helped close the remaining loop holes.[22] By the end of King Mohammed VI's first dozen years, the legal framework and regulatory regime had been strengthened sufficiently to provide the necessary tools to combat corruption.

Nevertheless, over the past two decades – despite the legal and institutional improvements – Moroccans continue to grow frustrated with the persistent unemployment, poverty, and inequality across the country. Denoeux suggests that Morocco's political economy is "driven primarily by the logic of clientelism and patronage,"[23] and Chayes, in testimony before the US Senate Foreign Relations Committee in 2016, identified Morocco as one of over 60 countries where corruption is "widespread and systemic."[24]

While analysts have focused on its pervasive and systemic nature, Moroccans have seen its practical and direct effect on their development. Morocco has consistently scored poorly on development indicators like the UN's HDI, which looks beyond large macroeconomic figures and factors in the "human face." These include, among other indicators, a country's health and education sectors in addition to its economic sector.

Morocco has shown positive signs on indicators like high immunization and primary school enrollment, as well as positive economic indicators like low inflation and low debt.[25] And since 1990, life expectancy has increased by almost ten years and the expected years of schooling and mean years of schooling have doubled.[26] Yet over that same span, the GNI per capita trend has remained relatively flat.[27]

Meanwhile, on any number of other indicators, difficult hurdles still remain. Morocco still falls well below the average Arab state and consistently ranks second to last in the region on its HDI score.[28] In health, Morocco's average rate of infant mortality and under-five mortality (an average of 25 deaths per 1,000) are concerning compared to peer countries like Tunisia that average 11 deaths per 1,000, despite similar life expectancy.[29] In education, Morocco's adult literacy (69.4%) is inadequate for effective economic development, particularly with the expansion of information technologies.[30] This problem is perpetuated by the low enrollment in secondary education (70%),[31] leaving the King to lament in 2013, "It's sad to note that the state of education is worse now than it was 20 years ago."[32]

And Morocco's inability to provide quality healthcare and education accessible to all Moroccans has affected the country's economic development. The unemployment rate has hovered around 10% due to a mismatch in skills and opportunities.[33] Too many Moroccans are under-educated or illiterate, leaving only a limited range of low-paying jobs available for possible employment. In response, Moroccan workers are hired to low-paying positions as a result of the high supply of untrained labor. For example, in 2016 and 2017, 67% of the new jobs were for rural positions that required less education.[34] But with only low-paying, low-skilled jobs available entrance into the middle class is difficult. Those who do receive an education have also suffered with high unemployment (25% among the college educated), due to the limited supply of well-paying jobs that match their skill and educational level.[35]

This, in part, explains the high unemployment among the youth (ages 15–24). Nearly 20% of Moroccan youth were unemployed in 2015, according to the United Nations, double the national rate.[36] However, in just two years, the Moroccan government was reporting that nearly 30% of youth were unemployed.[37] The high unemployment levels and limited availability of middle-class jobs have also perpetuated the persistently high rates of poverty. In 2007, 15% of the 31 million Moroccans lived in poverty.[38] In 2011, multidimensional poverty was 18.6%, according to the World Bank.[39] Morocco's export-oriented economy was certainly affected by the global downturn that began in 2007, and in response, the government launched the National Initiative for Human Development (INDH), which allocated $1.8 billion from 2011 to 2015 to increase literacy and reduce poverty.[40]

Struggling to enter the middle class, Moroccans have come to believe that in order to find work they need to know the right person. In Arabic, *Wasta*, which roughly translates as 'help through connections' or 'who you know,' is seen by Moroccans as necessary to get a job, even more than other Arab states.[41] As a Gallup poll from 2013 shows, nearly 80% of Moroccans believe that "knowing people in high positions is critical to get a job."[42] Not only is this one of the highest rates in the region – only behind Lebanon and Jordan – it can lead to dejection and reinforce a determinism that stymies the risk taking necessary for economic development. It can leave those without the "right" connections with a feeling of helplessness. It can affect business owners looking for financing or contracts as much as it can affect recent college graduates looking for their first job or a farmer moving to the city looking for more opportunity. And it perpetuates the divide between the haves and the have-nots.

The problem persists whether you are seeking a job in the private or public sector. While interviewing a former inspector in the Ministry of Finance, Chayes notes that the inspector said, "People have to be from the big families to get those [private sector] jobs. Those companies and the families that run them plan on breaking the law – participating in rigged tenders, handing out kickbacks. They can't have outsiders witnessing."[43] This harsh assessment by a former inspector validates the growing frustration among Moroccans who believe the government is only protecting the interests of the well-connected.

Moroccans feel like the system is not working for them and have begun to organize more protests in frustration over the lack of opportunity.[44] They feel the system is rigged and are increasingly willing to express that irritation. The online "Let it Spoil" campaign was sparked in April 2018 by frustration over recent price increases. The campaign called for the boycott of three companies: Afriquia gas stations, Sidi Ali bottled water, and Centrale Danone dairy products. Within two weeks, more than 90% of Moroccans were aware of the campaign and 70% between the ages of 15 and 24 and 31% over the age of 55 actively participated.[45] According to Mohammed Masbah, the director of the Moroccan Institute for Policy Analysis, the boycotters felt that each company's "strong links to the regime in Rabat" allowed them to acquire dominant market share and unfairly raise prices.[46] While other previous boycott campaigns led by Islamists or leftists failed to garner much attention, the campaign's wide appeal among a broad array of citizens indicates the country's growing resentment.[47]

"Let It Spoil" is an example of an increasingly exasperated citizenry. They have seen subsidies cut only to later discover that the fuel distributors' profits increased by billions of dirhams,[48] Uber leave because "Taxi Hawks" chased them out,[49] miners die while government officials profited,[50] and the government force telecommunications companies to cut advertising campaigns with media organizations that take too critical a stance toward the government.[51] Moroccans have also seen the selling of state resources under market value; selective regulation, tax breaks, and subsidies; and preferential government investment.

US State Department cables, released by WikiLeaks in 2009, provide another example. In one cable, a Moroccan businessman described how the King's holding company used its power to freeze the businessman's $220 million real estate deal since it was not included in the project.[52]

The vice president of the holding company reportedly told Qatari interlocutors that Morocco's major investment decisions were made by just three men: Fouad El Himma, counselor to the King and former head of the Party of Authenticity and Modernity; Mohamed Mounir Al Majidi, private secretary for the King and chief executive officer of SIGER (another holding company of the King); and the King; and "To have discussions with anyone else would be a waste of time."[53] This is not the first time Mounir Majidi has been mentioned in a questionable real estate deal either. Over a decade ago, while still in his same role, Majidi was accused of influencing the former Minister of Religious Endowments and Islamic Affairs Ahmed Tawfiq to sell him valuable real estate in Taroudant at one-ninetieth the market price.[54] Yet despite the credible allegations, Majidi maintains a significant leadership role overseeing the royal family's private holding company Société Nationale d'Investissement or National Investment Company (SNI).

The SNI has significant holdings in a variety of sectors including telecommunications, construction, mining, agriculture, energy, and banking including Attijariwafa Bank, the largest bank in Morocco. These sectors also happen to be some of the most profitable in Morocco's economy. Based on research from Cristina Corduneanu-Huci, this may be because, "firms in sectors with low rent potential are more likely to coordinate, claim, and obtain better governance in exchange for taxes, whereas high-rent companies find it difficult to sustain effective pro-governance collective action."[55] It also helps explain why Forbes ranks King Mohammed VI as the fifth richest man in Africa with a net worth of $5.7 billion.[56] But most importantly, it crowds out Moroccan SMEs who are unable to compete and perpetuates concerns of a rigged system.

Morocco also maintains a significant informal economy where citizens hope to earn at least a meager living. The Rif protests of 2016 were sparked by Mouhcine Fikri, a fish vendor operating informally and violating fishing regulations before he tragically died in a garbage truck.[57] But not all of the unregulated economy is small scale. Over a decade ago, the production and export of cannabis was thought to be a $10 billion industry in Morocco leading to extensive money laundering and the bribery of judges, police and customs officers, and public prosecutors. And with the improvements in communication and transportation, harder drugs entered Moroccan ports on their way to Europe, which led to the introduction of anti-money laundering and asset declaration laws mentioned above.[58] It has even been reported that the Makhzen and some royals may have been engaged in the drug trade.[59]

The informal economy's operation helps further deteriorate the authority and confidence in the state. While 90% of Moroccans are satisfied with the government's performance providing security, only 21% believe that their political leaders are concerned with ordinary citizens.[60] In addition, significant majorities of Moroccans remain dissatisfied with the government's performance in creating job opportunities (83%), addressing educational needs (58%), improving basic health services (68%), and keeping prices down (88%).[61]

Such perceptions fuels the disenchantment of citizens who see two systems in operation; not an informal and formal economy, but one where Majidi operates with impunity and the other where Fikri loses his life trying to provide for his family. And the inequality-adjusted HDI substantiates Moroccans' feelings of a division between the haves and the have-nots dropping 30% from .662 to .462 when adjusted for inequality.[62]

During the Arab Spring, the King's immediate and mostly peaceful response appeared to show a willingness to address the concerns of the protesters, giving many a sense of renewed hope. But after years of waiting for the implementation of reform, Moroccans appear to be growing increasingly frustrated over the lack of equal opportunity and vast disparities in wealth. Beginning in 2016, Moroccans again took to the streets in protest. Initially focused in the Rif region, the Hirak Movement quickly spread to other parts of the country. The protests were sparked when the 31-year-old Fikri was killed after he jumped into a garbage truck to try to salvage his confiscated swordfish in al-Hoceima.[63] But the movement's messages denouncing "rampant corruption, poor governance, and outright appropriation of the nation's resources," resonated with Moroccans across the country who were experiencing many of the same socioeconomic concerns.[64]

Increasingly, the protests over the past few years have drawn attention to the country's corruption, and inequality. Discontent is growing as Moroccan citizens do not see their concerns adequately addressed. But Morocco's problems are not the inadequacy of its laws and regulations. And the King has not been afraid to speak to the issue directly and put the weight of the throne behind anti-corruption efforts. In the King's Throne Day speech in 2016, he noted,

> Corruption is not inevitable and has never been part of Moroccan nature. However, it has become so commonplace that society considers it normal…Fighting corruption is a cause championed by both the State and society. The State, with all its institutions, has to fight this dangerous trend through the appropriate legal mechanisms and by incriminating all its aspects and severely punishing those involved in it.[65]

Government ministers have followed the King's lead. Saad Eddine El Othmani, prime minister of Morocco and secretary-general of the Justice and Development Party (PJD), noted in February 2018 during the 3rd Inter-Parliamentary Forum on Social Justice that, "combating administrative and financial corruption is a gateway for the realization of social justice, because of its great role in strengthening development and strengthening equity."[66] The PJD initially capitalized on Moroccan's frustrations following the Arab Spring, calling for the "moralization of the public and public institutions."[67] But since 2011 and despite the rhetoric of the King and other government officials, Moroccans feel little has changed.

The King has separated the monarchy from the dirtiness of day-to-day politics and governing, which has insulated him from much of the dissatisfaction.[68] The dismal polling numbers parliament and political parties receive reflects where the current blame is placed.[69] However, the direction of that frustration is not destined to remain this way. Rif protesters have begun dismissing political leaders as ineffective, only willing to engage with a delegation appointed by the King.[70] And some protesters marking the eighth anniversary of the Arab Spring in Morocco diverted from the main protest and headed toward a royal palace before being forcefully stopped by police.[71] Meanwhile, a song *"Fbladi Dalmouni"* has been viewed more than 6.5 million times on YouTube since its release in 2017.[72] The lyrics identify frustrations like government funds spent on mega projects rather than on social services and has evolved from an ode to its favorite soccer club sung by thousands of fans at soccer matches to a rallying cry for Moroccans expressing their discontent.[73]

In addition, Moroccans have largely viewed the Kingdom's reinstitution of compulsory military service as a response to quell the growing dissatisfaction among the youth rather than a legitimate national security concern. According to Smail Hamoudi, professor at the Faculty of Law in Settat, despite the government's argument that military service is needed to strengthen nationalism and offer access to trainings and other professional opportunities, the effect "will be…limited in scope, given that the social and economic challenges, especially the problem of youth unemployment, are bigger than a law or measure."[74]

The disenchantment Moroccans feel toward their political leadership may not bode well for the Kingdom's image of stability.[75] Confidence in Moroccan institutions is necessary to entice more domestic and international investment. And therein lies the ultimate challenge in Morocco's efforts to expand its economic development. It must find a way to create an economic environment that provides confidence and adequate opportunity for all Moroccans, not just the well-connected. Some industries have begun to see growth for Morocco's SMEs, like the integration of the local auto industry into the global value chain. But clearly more is needed to be done to create an inclusive environment that lifts more out of poverty and into the middle class and eliminates the divide between the haves and the have-nots.

Notes

1 United Nations, *Human Development Reports* (2018) Statistical Update. (United Nations Development Programme) Retrieved from http://hdr.undp.org/en/2018-update.
2 World Bank. (n.d.). *World Development Indicators Country Profile: Morocco* (Data). Retrieved February 1, 2019, from https://databank.worldbank.org/data/views/reports/reportwidget.aspx?Report_Name=CountryProfile&Id=b450fd57&tbar=y&dd=y&inf=n&zm=n&country=MAR.
3 Carothers, T., & Carothers, C. (2018, July 24). The One Thing Modern Voters Hate Most. *Foreign Policy*. Retrieved from https://foreignpolicy.com/2018/07/24/the-one-thing-modern-voters-hate-most-corruption/
4 Ibid.

5 Mc Lymont, F. (2018, October 26). Perceptions of Doing Business in Africa: The IGD Roadshow. *Africa Strictly Business*. Retrieved from https://www. africastrictlybusiness.com/perceptions-of-doing-business-in-africa-the-igd-roadshow/.

6 Aourraz, R. (2018, December 7). Stalled Liberalization: How the Rentier Economy Ousted Uber from Morocco. *Moroccan Institute for Policy Analysis*. Retrieved from https://mipa.institute/6220.

7 Ibid.

8 Ibid.

9 Ibid.

10 Denoeux, G. P. (2007). Corruption in Morocco: Old Forces, New Dynamics and a Way Forward. *Middle East Policy*, 14(4), 134–151. Retrieved from http:// search.ebscohost.com.proxy1.library.jhu.edu/login.aspx?direct=true&db= ijh&AN=58.7190&site=ehost-live&scope=site (p. 134).

11 Chayes, S. (2015). *Thieves of State: Why Corruption Threatens Global Security.* New York: W.W. Norton & Company, p. 70.

12 Arab Barometer. (2017, May 8). *Morocco Five Years after the Arab Uprisings* (Rep.). Retrieved from http://www.arabbarometer.org/wp-content/uploads/ Morocco_Public_Opinion_Survey_2016.pdf (p. 3).

13 Ibid.

14 Transparency International. (2018, February 21). *Corruptions Perception Index 2017* (Data). Retrieved from https://www.transparency.org/news/feature/ corruption_perceptions_index_2017?gclid=EAIaIQobChMI1M3e573S4AIV1Iu zCh1REgxrEAAYASAAEgJXjvD_BwE#table.

15 Transparency International. (2017, November 14). *Global Corruption Barometer: Citizens' Voices from Around the World* (Data). Retrieved January 5, 2019, from https://www.transparency.org/news/feature/global_corruption_barometer_ citizens_voices_from_around_the_world.

16 Transparency International. (n.d.). What Is Corruption? Retrieved February 2, 2019, from https://www.transparency.org/what-is-corruption?gclid=EAIaIQob ChMIiPnm_tnR3AIVno2zCh3z4wFSEAAYASAAEgJ_OvD_BwE#define.

17 Denoeux, G. P. (2007). Corruption in Morocco: Old Forces, New Dynamics and a Way Forward, p. 141.

18 United Nations. (2003, October 31). *Convention against Corruption*. Retrieved from https://treaties.un.org/doc/Treaties/2003/12/20031209 02-50 PM/Ch_XVIII_ 14p.pdf.

19 Denoeux, G. P. (2007). Corruption in Morocco: Old Forces, New Dynamics and a Way Forward, p. 140.

20 Ibid.

21 Al-Dadah, E., & Brillaud, F. (n.d.). Morocco: Pressing for Progress on Anticorruption. *The World Bank*. Retrieved February 2, 2019, from http:// siteresources.worldbank.org/INTMNAREGTOPGOVERNANCE/Resources/ dahdahandbrillaud.pdf.

22 Denoeux, G. P. (2007). Corruption in Morocco: Old Forces, New Dynamics and a Way Forward, p. 141.

23 Ibid., p. 134.

24 Chayes, S. (2016, June 30). *Corruption- Violent Extremism, Kleptocracy, and the Dangers of Failing Governance* (Congressional Testimony). Retrieved from https://www.foreign.senate.gov/imo/media/doc/063016_Chayes_Testimony.pdf.

25 United Nations, *Human Development Indicators: Morocco* (2018). (United Nations Development Programme). Retrieved from http://hdr.undp.org/en/ countries/profiles/MAR.

26 United Nations, *Human Development Indices and Indicators: 2018 Statistical Update Morocco* (2018). (United Nations Development Programme). Retrieved from http://hdr.undp.org/sites/all/themes/hdr_theme/country-notes/MAR.pdf.

27 Ibid.
28 Ibid.
29 United Nations, *Human Development Indicators: Morocco* (2018)
30 Ibid.
31 Ibid.
32 Alami, A. (2013, September 29). Gaps in Graduates' Skills Confounds Morocco. *New York Times.* Retrieved from https://www.nytimes.com/2013/09/30/world/africa/gaps-in-graduates-skills-confound-morocco.html.
33 The World Factbook: Morocco. (2018, February 1). Retrieved January 4, 2019, from https://www.cia.gov/library/publications/the-world-factbook/geos/mo.html.
34 Unemployment in Morocco: Young Urbans Have It the Worst in 2017. (2017, November 9). *Morocco World News.* Retrieved from https://www.moroccoworldnews.com/2017/11/233471/unemployment-morocco-young-urbans/.
35 http://www.universityworldnews.com/article.php?story=20160212082246110
36 http://hdr.undp.org/en/countries/profiles/MAR
37 Unemployment in Morocco: Young Urbans Have It the Worst in 2017. (2017, November 9).
38 The World Factbook: Morocco. (2018, February 1).
39 United Nations. (n.d.). Population in Multidimensional Poverty, Headcount (%) (for the Year of the Survey). Retrieved November 17, 2018, from http://hdr.undp.org/en/indicators/38606.
40 National Initiative for Human Development. (n.d.). Framing Budgetary. Retrieved January 5, 2019, from http://www.indh.ma/index.php/en/gouvernance-et-financement/cadrage-budgetaire.
41 Alaref, J. (2014, March 13). Wasta Once Again Hampering Arab Youth Chances for a Dignified Life [Web blog post]. Retrieved from http://blogs.worldbank.org/arabvoices/wasta-hampering-arab-youth-chances-dignified-life.
42 Ibid.
43 Chayes, S. (2015). *Thieves of State: Why Corruption Threatens Global Security,* p. 71.
44 Amos, D. (2012, January 27). In Morocco, Unemployment Can Be A Full-Time Job. *National Public Radio.* Retrieved from https://www.npr.org/2012/01/27/145860575/in-morocco-unemployment-can-be-a-full-time-job
45 Masbah, M. (2018, December 6). "Let It Spoil!": Morocco's Boycott and the Empowerment of 'Regular' Citizen. *Moroccan Institute for Policy Analysis.* Retrieved from https://mipa.institute/6216.
46 Ibid.
47 Ibid.
48 Ibid.
49 Aourraz, R. (2018, December 7). Stalled Liberalization: How the Rentier Economy Ousted Uber from Morocco.
50 Agence France-Presse. (2017, December 28). Thousands Protest in Morocco after Brothers Die in Illicit Coal Mine and Anger Rises to the Surface. *South China Morning Post.* Retrieved from https://www.scmp.com/news/world/africa/article/2125969/thousands-protest-morocco-after-brothers-die-illicit-coal-mine-and.
51 Bouziane Zaid (2017) The Authoritarian Trap in State/Media Structures in Morocco's Political Transition. *The Journal of North African Studies,* 22(3), 340–360. doi:10.1080/13629387.2017.1307910 (p. 346).
52 Palace Coercion Plagues Morocco's Real Estate Sector. (2009, December 11). *WikiLeaks.* Retrieved from https://wikileaks.org/plusd/cables/09CASABLANCA226_a.html.
53 Ibid.
54 Denoeux, G. P. (2007). Corruption in Morocco: Old Forces, New Dynamics and a Way Forward, p. 138.

55 Corduneanu-Huci, C. (2016). Taming Corruption: Rent Potential, Collective Action, and Taxability in Morocco. *Business and Politics*, 18(3), 297–335. https://www.cambridge.org/core/journals/business-and-politics/all-issues (p. 298).
56 #5 King Mohammed VI. (2015, November 18). *Forbes*. Retrieved from https://www.forbes.com/profile/king-mohammed-vi/#9c2d08b1c93a.
57 Alami, A. (2016, October 30). Protests Erupt in Morocco over Fish Vendor's Death in Garbage Compactor. *New York Times*. Retrieved from https://www.nytimes.com/2016/10/31/world/middleeast/protests-erupt-in-morocco-over-fish-vendors-death-in-garbage-compactor.html.
58 Ketterer, J. (2001). Networks of Discontent in Northern Morocco. *Middle East Research and Information Project*. Retrieved from https://merip.org/2001/03/networks-of-discontent-in-northern-morocco/.
59 Ibid.
60 Arab Barometer. (2017, May 8). *Morocco Five Years after the Arab Uprisings*, p. 1.
61 Ibid., p. 7.
62 United Nations, *Inequality-Adjusted HDI (IHDI)*. (2018). (United Nations Development Programme). Retrieved from http://hdr.undp.org/en/indicators/138806.
63 Alami, A. (2016, October 30). Protests Erupt in Morocco over Fish Vendor's Death in Garbage Compactor.
64 El Malki, F. (2017, June 2). Morocco's Hirak Movement: The People versus the Makhzen. *Jadaliyya*. Retrieved from http://www.jadaliyya.com/Details/34330/Morocco's-Hirak-Movement-The-People-Versus-the-Makhzen.
65 Full Text of Royal Speech on Throne Day. (2016, July 30). *Ministry of Culture and Communication*. Retrieved from http://www.maroc.ma/en/royal-activities/full-text-royal-speech-throne-day.
66 Morocco Still Struggles Against Corruption, Government Accelerating Reform Efforts: El Othmani. (2018, February 19). *Morocco World News*. Retrieved from https://www.moroccoworldnews.com/2018/02/240949/morocco-corruption-government-reform-saad-eddine-el-othmani/.
67 Wegner, E. (2011). *Islamist Opposition in Authoritarian Regimes: The Party of Justice and Development in Morocco*. Syracuse: Syracuse University Press, p. 102.
68 F. Gregory Gause III, "Kings for All Seasons: How the Middle East's Monarchies Survived the Arab Spring," Brookings Doha Center, Analysis Paper Number 8 (2013), p. 25.
69 Arab Barometer. (2017, May 8). *Morocco Five Years after the Arab Uprisings*, p. 6.
70 Masbah, M. (2018, July 30). What Protest in Morocco Reveal about Public Trust in Political Parties. *Moroccan Institute for Policy Analysis*. Retrieved from https://mipa.institute/5834.
71 El-Masaiti, A. (2019, February 20). Morocco: Arab Spring Anniversary Brings Reflection, Beatings. *Associated Press*. Retrieved from https://www.abc4.com/news/world-news/moroccan-police-crack-down-on-protesting-teachers/1795823001.
72 Gruppo Aquile: F'Bladi Delmouni. (2017, March 27). Retrieved February 20, 2019, from https://www.youtube.com/watch?v=kJvFAUZiK-Q.
73 Alami, A. (2018, December 20). The Soccer Politics of Morocco. *The New York Review of Books*. Retrieved from https://www.nybooks.com/daily/2018/12/20/the-soccer-politics-of-morocco/.
74 Hamoudi, S. (2019, February 11). Morocco's Return to Compulsory Military Service: Reasons and Challenges. *Moroccan Institute for Policy Analysis*. Retrieved from https://mipa.institute/6451.
75 (Mis) Trust and the Quality of Political and Economic Institutions (2019, February 11). *Moroccan Institute for Policy Analysis*. Retrieved from https://mipa.institute/6391.

7 Developing Morocco's tourism sector and gaining greater market share

When King Mohammed VI assumed Morocco's throne in 1999, travel and tourism accounted for 11% of the country's gross domestic product (GDP).[1] In 2017, travel and tourism in Morocco was equal to 18.6% of GDP.[2] In 1999, this was equal to $4.7 billion.[3] In 2017, tourism and travel was equal to $20 billion in current prices.[4] Morocco's tourism industry has increased annually with the exception of the years 2009, 2012, and 2015. The downturn in 2009 reflected the world economic recession from the banking scandals in the West and the decline in 2012 reflected tourists' concerns about the Arab Spring. The 2015 decline was more sector specific, reflecting mainly shorter stays by tourists but also a response to fears in the aftermath of the Paris attacks by terrorists.[5] In 2011, Morocco's tourist sector employed 886,100 workers, its highest year ever for employment. In 2017, 818,000 workers were employed in the sector.[6] Additionally, Morocco has been able to attract much-needed foreign investment that it had aspired to attract to develop its tourist sector. In recent years, however, when the sector ultimately did not attain its ambitious goals, foreign investment stalled. Tourists continue, however, to provide Morocco with foreign exchange through their purchases and hospitality bookings.

When viewed by economic and employment indicators, under King Mohammed VI, Morocco's tourism sector has been a development success even though it has fallen short of attaining all of its goals. In the second decade of Mohammed VI's reign, however, non-economic issues also came to the fore. As discussed later in this chapter, with the increasing political success of Morocco's Islamic party (the Justice and Development Party (PJD)), regulations in the tourism sector became one site for struggles over cultural values and freedom of action between religious Members of Parliament and more secular Moroccan administrators who wanted to protect Morocco's tourism success. Additionally, while the tourism sector has been one driver of Morocco's development, similarly to the agricultural sector which is Morocco's largest employer of Moroccans, the tourism sector is partially dependent on external variables. Success in the agricultural sector requires a proper mix of sun and rain while success in the tourism sector requires political peace and the defeat of terrorism.

Additionally, while "Vision 2020," Morocco's second tourism sector plan under Mohammed VI, has brought many improvements to Morocco, two of the plan's goals – keep maintain national authenticity or "genuineness" and to achieve environmental sustainability – continue to need work. There are important trades-offs among the economic, environmental, and political/social impact that tourism brings to a community. By 2019, it appeared that Morocco's leaders needed to pay closer attention to these trade-offs, especially those that involve water usage. Further, while Morocco's popular tourist attractions that held cultural landmarks gained new tourists, more hospitality workers in remote areas of Morocco with cultural landmarks saw some increase in tourism but not nearly as much as they had hoped.

For Morocco's tourism sector to truly succeed, the country will need to improve its overall development. Rankings of tourism competitiveness point to some areas in which Morocco must improve and these areas, in turn, depend on development achievements that are not simply related to tourism. The World Economic Forum's Travel and Tourism Competitiveness Report 2017 ranked Morocco third (after South Africa and Mauritius) in Africa; Morocco was ranked 65th out of 136 countries.[7] The country's weaknesses included an evaluation of the health and hygiene category for which Morocco was ranked 99 of 136. And Morocco was ranked 77 of 136 in the information and communications technology (ICT) readiness category.[8] Health, hygiene, and technology are issues to which tourists pay attention.

Under Mohammed VI's father, King Hassan II, Morocco's tourism patterns included those who mainly sought three areas of Morocco: the beaches on the Bay of Agadir; the Imperial Cities, usually Meknes, Marrakesh, Fez, and sometimes Rabat (the 12th century Imperial City of the Almohad dynasty); and the Route of the Ksour and Kasbahs in which visitors explore "fortified villages, houses, and granaries built of pisé, a sun dried mixture of mud and clay" that that are found along the Erfoud –Ouarzazate road through the Dadés valley (especially the Agdz-Zagora portion of the road).[9] Tourists provided much-needed foreign exchange.

After assuming the throne in 1999, King Mohammed VI and his advisors quickly recognized the potential economic benefits for Morocco that expanding the country's tourism sector could provide. Thus, in 2001, Morocco began to implement a strategic plan for the tourist sector called "Vision 2010." Morocco's tourism sector earns billions, as noted above, and expanding tourism would secure even more precious foreign exchange for Morocco to use to develop its other sectors. The tourism sector also provides jobs requiring a range of skills and the sector has a ripple effect across the economy. Those employed within the tourist sector as hotel clerks, cleaners, restaurant servers, accountants, etc., are joined by independent workers outside of the hotels who are dependent on the tourists' trade. Many of those working in building construction who remodel shops located near tourist hotels, as well as the owners of those shops and their shop clerks are dependent on tourism. Those working in restaurants near hotels or tourist attractions and those working in travel agencies and transport also are employees who benefit from tourism. The World Travel & Tourism Council reported that in 2016, the total contribution of the tourism sector to Morocco was 16.6% of total employment or 1,902,500 jobs; the numbers for 2017 (the latest available) were expected to increase to 1,907,500 jobs.[10]

Additionally, about 40% of Moroccans work in Morocco's largest sector, the agricultural sector, and these workers also benefit from Morocco's tourists. The more food that Moroccans can produce for its tourists, the more protected it is from global market competition. Additionally, more earned revenue can be kept in the country if agricultural producers do not have to pay the shipping costs to move their products abroad or pay tariffs to the market country.

To facilitate the development of the tourism industry, Morocco had to build new hotels and upgrade its interface with global communications. It had to improve its roads, its trains, and its airports. The chapter on Morocco's transportation demonstrates that its transportation sector improvements allowed tourists entering Morocco to enjoy world class 21st century travel even as they visited medieval Berber castles or Moroccan ruins dating to the time of the Romans.

Morocco's first tourism plan was, for the most part, well executed and by 2011 at the end of the plan, Morocco ranked 25th as a tourist destination globally. In 1999, tourism and travel provided 5% of Morocco's total employment.[11] In 2017, it provided 7.1% of Moroccan jobs.[12] Although the King had hoped to attract tourists in even greater numbers, the sector is considered a successful component of the country's economic development during Mohammed VI's reign. It was reported that 93% of its goals had been met.[13]

Building on the first ten years of success, Morocco created a new plan, "Vision 2020: Stratégie De Développement Touristique (Strategy for Tourism Development)" to guide the tourist industry for the second decade of Mohamed VI's reign. But optimism for achieving all of its targets was tempered due to the regional unrest that affected the perceptions of possible tourists considering a trip to a Middle East and North African country. In an interview with Marie-Beatrice Lallemand, General Manager of Morocco's Mazagan Beach Resort, this concern was evident. The interviewer noted that "In 2010 Morocco received 9.5 million visitors which was 12 percent growth from the year before."[14] Lallemand responded that

> 2010 was a good year and very successful if you consider where Morocco was coming from. Mazagan was also very successful and we achieved over 50 percent occupancy in the first year of operation. Unfortunately 2011 will be impacted by the events in North Africa and Mazagan has lo(s)t many groups and conferences due to the situation.[15]

Lallemand also noted that Morocco itself was well placed to offer a range of activities for tourists who lived close to Morocco but overlooked its offerings:

> Morocco is a country with a rich history and tradition. The climate is so diverse so there is a lot to do. Morocco is less than three hours away from most of Europe and for a long time the French have been aware of this but the other European countries didn't realize this.[16]

However, Lallemand also indicated that all the obstacles to expanding tourism were not beyond Morocco's control; she also noted:

> it is time to do something with communication and things are starting to happen now. There definitely is a will to get all the players in Morocco together and on the same page working together.[17]

In 2010, to oversee the new plan and its initiatives in tourism, Yassir Znagui was appointed to serve as Minister of Tourism in the government led by the Istiqlal Party and its Prime Minister, Abbas El Fassi. Yassir Znagui was born in 1970. That the King and his Prime Minister were choosing young leaders was new for Morocco and telling for the sector. As Znagui noted,

> I am the Minister of Tourism and my colleague, the Minister of Youth and Sport, is my age. Another colleague who is almost our age is the Minister of Transports and Infrastructure. In addition to that, we have the chance to have a very young, open-minded and dynamic King. This obviously creates a strong dynamic in the country, but it is not enough – we need more youth in the political system and the economic one...[18]

During an interview with the new Minister of Tourism, Yassir Znagui, the reporter asked whether Morocco might benefit from tourists who were avoiding Egypt and Tunisia. Znagui replied that this was not part of Morocco's plan. Morocco would simply continue to build on its own strengths. He noted that "We have not been going out in the media saying that we are better off or that we are more stable" out of respect to Morocco's neighbors.[19] Moreover, Znagui noted that in 2010, Morocco was attracting a particular kind of tourist:

> 70% of tourism in Morocco is spontaneous – people booking directly via websites or directly with hotel operators. We also have what we call in the industry last minute booking. 30% of the 70% is last minute booking, meaning the last week; the second 30% is the last month. This is a completely different model than the neighboring countries' where they mainly have tour operating tourism and low cost mass tourism.

Therefore, today we are not in the position to catch all the flows leaving Tunisia and Egypt. We see them leaving to other destinations like the Canary Islands. [20]

It is clear that early in 2010, Moroccans with responsibilities in the tourist industry were keenly aware of the challenges and opportunities that they faced due to politics in the region and their niche in the global market.

But then in March and April 2011, Morocco experienced widespread demonstrations similar to those in other Middle Eastern countries and many worried this truly would undermine the country's tourist trade. Morocco's monarch, however, acted swiftly and promised some reforms to the political sector as well as to the economic well-being of the country. A new constitution was created and, when national elections were held, a new government under the new constitution took office on November 29, 2011. The new government was led by a new Prime Minister, Abdelilah Benkirane, leader of the Islamic religious party, the PJD, which had won the most seats in the National Assembly in the country's national elections.

In the new government's cabinet, the new Minister of Tourism was a Member of Parliament who had been elected on the Popular Movement (MP) platform, a party that holds appeal in the rural areas and traditionally has supported the King. Lahcen Haddad was appointed the new Minister of Tourism on January 3, 2012. And though not quite as young as the previous Minister, Yassir Znagui (Haddad was just a decade older), Haddad was still considered young for a leadership position in Morocco when viewed alongside past ministers who served in various capacities.

When Haddad took over the tourism sector, he faced the challenges of unrest noted above, but additionally he faced some difficult technological challenges as well. One component of the Vision 2010 plan was known as the Azur initiative and it was designed to develop six coastal resorts. Unfortunately, that was one component of the Vision 2010 plan that had not been achieved. When Haddad was asked about how he might improve the Agadir region's tourism prospects, he noted that a priority in the new tourist strategy would be to promote "growth areas" and also to provide support for improvements in air-related links to tourism.[21] He also noted that the "revival of the seaside resort also involves accompanying measures to upgrade the hotel fleet."[22] So, it is clear that both new conveniences for air travel and modern hospitality accommodations had to be adopted if Morocco was to be competitive and also develop its potential growth areas, such as Agadir.

"Vision 2010" had established the goal of attracting ten million visitors to Morocco. Morocco attracted 9.3 million tourists and "Vision 2010" was considered a success even though it fell a bit shy of its numerical goal. "Vision 2020" set a goal of 18 million visitors by the year 2020, and the King noted that he would like to see the country in the top 20 destinations for tourists.[23]

New target populations for Moroccan tourism were identified from the United States, Russia, and China through promotions of group tours, as well as targeting the spontaneous visitors coming from those countries.[24] Additionally, the King and his ministers would continue to support the growth of the hotel industry with guarantees of improved infrastructure and easy credit for foreign investors.[25] But even in 2011, critics began to warn that while world-class luxury hotels (Four Seasons, Hyatt, Best Western, Raffles, Accor, Ibis, Hilton and Kenzi, etc.) had begun operations in "Marrakech, Casablanca, Agadir, Rabat, Tangier and El Jadida, there is a need for brand-name budget-style accommodation" as well.[26] As the new Tourism Minister, Haddad also gave attention to tourists from Germany:

> I am convinced that we could do better because this country provides a significant number of tourists (70,000) with high purchasing power. This country stands out as well for its proximity to Morocco. We need then to double up our efforts with respect to Germany.[27]

Promotion became a new focus of the Ministry of Tourism. To attract new tourists, Morocco opened representative offices in Russia (Moscow), Sweden (Stockholm), and Poland (Bratislava).

To be certain that Moroccan tourist destinations planned for both foreign and domestic travelers, new local planning groups were to be established. Additionally, eight target tourist destinations and six framework programs were identified. The tourist destinations included Marrakech and the Atlantic, Central Atlantic, Northern Cape, Mediterranean Morocco, the Centre of Morocco, Atlas and the Valleys, Souss Sahara Atlantic, and the Great Southern Atlantic Coast. The six framework programs included The Azur 2020; Patrimony and Heritage; Events, Sport and Leisure; High Value-Added Niche Programs of Business and Well-Being; Biladi; and the Green/Eco/Sustainable Development program.[28]

One of the major programs of the plan was to develop, by 2020, ten tourist destinations in Morocco – for Moroccans – called Biladi, or "my country" in Arabic. To accomplish this, hotels for (many) Moroccans would need to offer a different price point than many of the luxury hotels for foreigners. But this presented a dilemma. When the international economy was constrained or when oil prices drove up airline tickets, five-star hotels attractive to mostly foreign nationals retained a national occupancy rate of 60%–73%, while more modestly priced hotels retained only a 45% occupancy rate.[29] The Ministry of Tourism was going to have to plan for less highly ranked hotels while continuing to upgrade accommodations for foreigners in more expensive hotels.

The tourist sector's new "Vision 2020" also offered a strategy that concentrated on "genuineness" or authenticity to make Morocco an attractive destination.[30] To accomplish this, it was reported that "The ministry will take on preemptive measures to protect Morocco's natural and cultural heritages to reinforce Morocco's cultural identity."[31] And it is through public-private partnerships that Morocco hoped to complete anywhere from 300 to 400 projects for tourism across Morocco.[32] Such projects would include ecological sites, museums, and houses, restaurants, gas stations, and small clubs. The Vision 2020 plan called for doubling the number of tourist arrivals and tripling the number of domestic trips.[33]

Of great importance for many, "Vision 2020" also included an environmental initiative as a major focus of the plan. "Vision 2020" offered a new emphasis on eco-tourism and sustainability. It sought to develop "a new generation of tourists products, long-term ecosystem management and local people's participation in development and the benefits of tourism."[34] For tourists, this included eco-lodges, desert resorts, and glamping (glamorous camping). The environmental component was seen as integrating sustained and responsible custody of the environment with respect for authentic social and cultural practices. Numerous sources note that necessity drives this concern. In practice, Morocco's hospitality centers are finding creative ways to conserve water, energy, and to recycle waste in a country where water and energy are scarce. Yet in 2014, a survey of hotel operators in the Souss-Massa-Dràa Region revealed that only a few of the tourist establishments in this region fulfilled the "legal requirements concerning the impact of their business on the environment."[35] Clearly, courses and workshops over the next years were necessary.

Planning also would be necessary for targeted destination areas at the local level. Metrics for monitoring tourist impact on the environment to determine the limits of tourist density would be critical. Baseline studies of natural habitat, monitoring tourists' water consumption, and energy use, as well as studies of local wastewater treatment capacities were required. Morocco's national leaders saw to it that environmental audits of the fragility of numerous ecosystems were conducted. This information was provided to the new, local tourist development agencies.

Another focus was also a key strategy of "Vision 2020." The "Vision 2020" plan included a new governance structure for monitoring and implementing Morocco's tourism strategy: tourism development agencies. At the local level, there would be eight tourism development agencies with various stakeholders participating in decision-making, and it was anticipated that perhaps local environmental nongovernmental organizations (NGOs) could help to play a role.

The idea of having decentralized tourist development agencies fits neatly with the larger plan of Morocco's decentralization of its political and economic development that has emerged over the years during the reign of Mohammed VI. More and more planning, regulatory responsibility, and implementation oversight have been shifted from the nation's capital to regional centers whose leaders have assumed more and more responsibilities for economic development:

> Regarding the tourism development agencies, Tourism Minister Haddad noted that: It takes a year or two to implement them effectively. They should also allow for concerted and shared governance and greater involvement at the local level.[36]

Simultaneously at the national level, a new governance structure for "Vision 2020" helped to create a High Tourism Authority that reported to the Prime Minister and which coordinated the Ministries of Tourism, Interior, Transportation, Culture, and Crafts.

To support the work of those at the multi-level tourist sector that Morocco was designing, new training and professional courses were offered. Moroccans at the national, regional, and local levels enrolled and gained skills to help ensure the plan's success. Those who did business in the sector were also encouraged to enroll in workshops or in courses. The new plans would require development experts, sports instructors, museum professionals, and human resources professionals to facilitate employment and benefits. A hospitality school of higher learning for each of the eight tourist areas was planned. It was believed that the curriculum and the activities of such a learning center would result from private–public partnerships because most of the activities in the region were to be developed and managed by small and big businesses in the private sector.[37] Additionally, Haddad sought regulatory reform of the tourist sector in four main arenas: tourist accommodations, travel agencies and organizations, tourist transportation, and tour guides. This required the identification of target behaviors and activities, a variety of professional trainings, and surprise inspections for hygiene and health.[38]

Morocco's collaboration with the United Nations Economic, Scientific and Cultural Organization (UNESCO) on its World Heritage Culture work also has benefited Morocco's tourist aspirations. Although Morocco had signed the World Heritage Convention as early as 1975 (the convention went into force in 1972) and a number of sites designated as World Heritage sites had already boosted Morocco's tourism sector, the Vision 2020 plan allowed Morocco to pursue planning for tourist visits to its sites in a much more intentional manner as part of its authenticity/genuine components design. In 2019, Morocco has nine sites already listed as World Heritage Cultural sites and 13 more pending following their application to UNESCO. The nine already designated UNESCO World Cultural sites include Archaeological Site of Volubilis (1997), the Historic City of Meknes (1996), Ksar of Ait-Ben-Haddou (1987), Medina of Essaouira (formerly Mogador) (2001), the Medina of Fez (1981), the Medina of Marrakesh (1985), the Medina of Tétouan (previously called Titawin) (1997), the Portuguese City of Mazagan (El Jadida) (2004), and Rabat, Morocco's political capital, and also a historic Imperial City (2012).

Lahcen Haddad was not only a politician but also a highly regarded academic and someone who also had administered several NGOs and so was familiar with small businesses and local NGO concerns. Haddad also was skilled in the use of social media. But Haddad had to face new challenges to the tourism sector that few other Ministers of Tourism must confront.

In the new Islamic party-led National Assembly, MPs from the governing PJD demanded that alcohol be banned in Morocco as it is forbidden for Muslims to drink alcohol. In the National Assembly, it was the task of the new Minister of Tourism to rebut this demand in the name of democracy and freedom of choice. Obviously, the numbers of tourists coming to Morocco would have dramatically declined if such a law had been passed.

Other struggles in the tourist sector with regard to religious practices also arose. For example, in 2014, some resorts in Marrakesh banned the wearing of "burkinis" also called a "halal swimsuit." A burkini is a swimming suit for modest Muslim women who want greater covering and so have suits with leggings and headscarves, etc. It was argued that the burkinis posed a hygiene risk for other users in the resorts' pools. A Member of Parliament, Abdelaziz Aftati, representing the religious PJD "sent a complaint to Tourism Minister Lahcen Haddad" and noted that such bans expressed the "rudeness of the new colonization."[39]

Then Haddad had to navigate other political waters when a gay cruise ship arrived at Casablanca for the final leg of a cruise that began in Barcelona and was to have been the first such visit to a Muslim country by a self-identified gay tour. But harbor authorities refused permission for the ship's passengers to disembark. In response, Haddad declared publicly to the press that such a decision had not been taken by the Moroccan government which, he argued, respects human rights.[40] The cruise ship returned to Spain. Although Haddad distanced the government from the event, the incident gave pause to other LGBT tour operators who might have contemplated a stop in Morocco.

Morocco's efforts to attract new tourists from China were improved when it was announced that in June 2016 Chinese tourists would no longer need a visa to enter Morocco.[41] King Mohammed VI and China's President Xi Jinping signed a number of accords in 2016 and one promised to expand tourism. At that time, it was estimated that about 15,000 Chinese tourists annually visited Morocco and Moroccans were hoping to push the number to 100,000 annually.[42] Indeed by the end of 2016, 43,000 Chinese tourists had visited Morocco.[43] And in 2018, 180,000 Chinese tourists visited Morocco.[44] Then, Mohamed Sajid, Morocco's Minister of Tourism, Air Transport, Handicraft and Social Economy, as the new cabinet position was named, announced that direct passenger flights between Morocco and China would commence "before the end of 2019."[45]

Morocco's Tourist Ministry was shuffled in April 2017. The former Mayor of Casablanca, Mohamed Sajid was appointed to the cabinet post. But in an effort to coordinate Tourism and Air Transit, the cabinet ministries were reorganized with Air Transit being brought into the former Tourism ministry along with Handicraft and Social Economy. And Sajid did indeed focus on transit projects already in the works, including flights between Marrakesh and Fez and European cities. It was hoped that the proposed new high-speed rail link between Tangier and Casablanca that was to cost $2 billion would also boost tourism. In fact, the high-speed rail was another leapfrog technology development initiative that King Mohammed VI was able to adopt. The speed line was known as "Al Boraq" and, when it opened for travel in December 2018 (after about a decade of construction), it was the first high-speed rail link on the African continent.[46]

Morocco had held elections in October 2016 but the former Prime Minister and leader of the PJD, the largest party in the National Assembly, could not persuade other parties to join him to form a majority coalition. Several of the parties in the previous coalition and loyal to the King were unwilling to accept Abdelilah Benkirane to continue as Prime Minister. But the PJD still possessed the greatest number of seats in the National Assembly. After about five months had passed, King Mohammed VI reached out to another leader of the PJD, Saâdeddine El Otmani, and chose him as Prime Minister instead of the increasingly independent and popular Benkirane. The impasse was broken.

In El Otmani's new government, Mohamed Sajid was appointed as the new Minister of Tourism, Air Transit, Handicraft and Social Economy in Morocco's cabinet. Sajid is said to be born in "1948 to Amazigh (Berber) parents from Taroudant."[47] He had served as a leading politician in Casablanca and was elected as a Member of Parliament on the Constitutional Union (UC) party platform. As noted above, he immediately began to conclude those transport projects that had been in the works for some time.

One of the new concerns in 2018 that arose for Morocco's new Minister was the steady increase in oil prices and consequently the increase in airfares to Morocco. By July 2018, as the government of Morocco was preparing its 2019 budget, it had to grapple with the effects of rising oil prices. The government expected lower numbers of travelers as transit costs increased; the cost of a barrel of oil had sold at $60 a barrel and now sold at $73 a barrel; Morocco's government also began to talk of protectionist measures to protect Moroccan industries.[48] Moroccan citizens were taking to the streets to protest outside oil and gas company delivery stations as well as boycotting some targeted companies.

Increases in transit costs also affect one other component of Morocco's tourism sector that it hoped to develop more fully. Vision 2020 also sought to increase Business tourism. Consequently, Meetings, Incentives, Conferences, and Exhibitions (MICE) facilities were targeted for expansion. For example, the United Nations Climate Change Conference was convened in Marrakech in November 2016. In October 2018, Marrakech hosted the Arab Energy Conference, the first time it was held in Morocco. In December 2018, Morocco hosted the 6th annual international renewable and sustainable energy conference in Rabat. Also in December 2018, Morocco hosted the United Nations Migration Compact Conference in Marrakech. In February 2019, Marrakech hosted the second annual Oil & Gas Summit. Also in February 2019, Rabat hosted the Euromoney Conference for Morocco in which international investors and government leaders gathered annually to analyze some aspect of the country's strategic financial concerns, in this year of Morocco's distinctive "pivot to Africa."

Morocco's tourist leaders hope that such business tourism helps Morocco to weather the vagaries of individual tourist choices and also burnish the county's reputation. And there is hope that attendees at such gatherings could well return as individual tourists with family and friends. And in Tangiers, where European industries, especially auto manufacturers, have a large presence, MICE is expected to play a major role in Tangiers' tourist profile.

In addition to pocketbook issues, a major concern of travelers over time, according to news reports, is a concern regarding terrorism and safety. And so even though Morocco continues to be one of the safest countries in the Middle East, the association of young Moroccans who have left the country and joined terrorist networks continues to give pause to the traveling public outside Morocco when it is mentioned that a terrorist is Moroccan. Additionally, the December 2018 beheadings of two (one Danish and one Norwegian) young women tourists have not helped Morocco's security profile and clearly frightened not only tourists but also those who hoped to enter Morocco for general study away programs and to study Arabic in Morocco. Such students from Europe and America often also spend weekends as tourists, or take time after their studies to travel as tourists.

"Vision 2020" in the tourism sector, like the development strategy favored by the King in other sectors, employed the use of public partnerships for development and also applied leapfrog practices after seeking the most advanced practices in eco-tourism and sustainability. A professionalization of those in the tourism industry was also promoted. Morocco's tourism sector continues to be a driver of employment and foreign exchange for Morocco but its success remains partially beyond the control of Moroccan planners. Oil prices and security issues continue to influence the fortunes of the sector. And Morocco's King Mohammed VI continues to diversify his target populations and the kind of tourists his country attracts in an effort to protect the sector from any one challenge.

Notes

1 Knoema Corporation. (n.d.). "Morocco – Contribution of Travel and Tourism to GDP as a Share of GDP". Retrieved February 23, 2019, from https://knoema.com/atlas/Morocco/topics/Tourism/Travel-and-Tourism-Total-Contribution-to-GDP/Contribution-of-travel-and-tourism-to-GDP-percent-of-GDP.
2 Ibid.
3 Knoema Corporation. (n.d.). "Morocco – Contribution of Travel and Tourism to GDP in Current Prices". Retrieved February 23, 2019, from https://knoema.com/atlas/Morocco/topics/Tourism/Travel-and-Tourism-Total-Contribution-to-GDP/Contribution-of-travel-and-tourism-to-GDP.
4 Ibid.
5 Morocco's tourist minister noted that "The sector faced the difficult global context as well as "the impact of the informal sector and shorter lengths of stay." Maroc.ma. (2015, December 21). "Global Context Impact on Tourism in Morocco, 'Mitigated' in 2015". Retrieved February 22, 2018, from http://www.maroc.ma/en/news/global-context-impact-tourism-morocco-mitigated-2015.

6 World Travel and Tourism Council, *Travel & Tourism Economic Impact 2017 Morocco*, p. 1.
7 The World Economic Forum's Travel and Tourism Competitiveness Report 2017. Retrieved March 1, 2019, from http://www3.weforum.org/docs/WEF_TTCR_2017_web_0401.pdf.
8 Ibid.
9 Stallings, D. ed. (2012). *Fodor's Morocco* (New York: Random House Inc.), p. 318.
10 Ibid. World Travel and Tourism Council, Travel & Tourism Economic Impact 2017 Morocco, p. 1.
11 Knoema Corporation. (n.d.). "Morocco – Direct Contribution of Travel and Tourism to Employment as a Share of GDP". Retrieved February 23, 2019, from https://knoema.com/atlas/Morocco/topics/Tourism/Travel-and-Tourism-Direct-Contribution-to-Employment/Direct-contribution-of-travel-and-tourism-to-employment-percent-of-GDP.
12 Ibid.
13 Ministry of Tourism and Crafts. (2010). Vision 2020: Stratégie De Développement Touristique, p. 24.
14 Marcopolis. (2011, March 31). "Morocco Destination: Successful Tourism Destination in Morocco". Retrieved February 12, 2019, from https://marcopolis.net/morocco-destination-sucessful-tourism-destination-in-morocco.htm.
15 Ibid.
16 Ibid.
17 Ibid.
18 Marcopolis. (2011, April 5). "Morocco Report Morocco's Ministry of Tourism: New Vision for Tourism in Morocco". Retrieved February 12, 2019, from https://marcopolis.net/moroccos-ministry-of-tourism-new-vision-for-tourism-in-morocco.htm.
19 Ibid.
20 Ibid.
21 Alami, M. (2012, February 21). "Les priorités de Lahcen Haddad, ministre du Tourisme". *L'Economiste*. Retrieved February 15, 2019, from https://www.maghress.com/fr/leconomiste/1891469.
22 Ibid.
23 Roudies, N. (2013, October 29). "Vision 2020 for Tourism in Morocco Focus on Sustainability and Ecotourism". Paper Presented at the Expert Group Meeting on Ecotourism, Poverty Reduction & Environmental Protection Retrieved February 15, 2019, from http://www.oecd.org/regional/leed/46761560.pdf OECD. Nada Roudies is the Secretary General Moroccan Ministry of Tourism.
24 Morocco.com. (2011, April 27)."Morocco's Hotel Industry Looks to the Future". Retrieved February 23, 2019, from https://www.morocco.com/blog/morocco-s-hotel-industry-looks-to-the-future/.
25 Ibid.
26 Ibid.
27 The World Folio. (2013). "A Cherished Tourist Destination". Retrieved March 2, 2019, from http://www.theworldfolio.com/interviews/lahcen-haddad-minister-of-tourism-of-morocco-n1573/1573/.
28 Op. cit. Roudies, N. "Vision 2020 for tourism in Morocco Focus on Sustainability and Ecotourism."
29 Ibid. The World Folio, "A Cherished Tourist Destination".
30 Mohamed Dekkak Blog 2016–2018. (n.d.). "Morocco's 2020 Vision and Plans for the Tourism Industry." Retrieved February 15, 2019, from https://dekkak.com/moroccos-tourism-industry/.
31 Ibid.

32 Op. cit. The World Folio, "A Cherished Tourist Destination".
33 Op. cit. Roudies, N. "Vision 2020 for Tourism in Morocco Focus on Sustainability and Ecotourism."
34 Ibid.
35 Kagermeier, A., Amzil, L., & Elfasskaoui, B. (2018). "Governance Aspects Of Sustainable Tourism In The Global South: Evidence from Morocco" in Jan Mosedale and Frieder Voll, eds., *Sustainability and Tourism: 25 years after Rio – and Now?* (Mannheim, Germany: MetaGIS).
36 Op. cit. Alami, M. "Les priorités de Lahcen Haddad, ministre du Tourisme."
37 Op. cit. The World Folio, "A Cherished Tourist Destination."
38 *Morocco World News.* (2016, August 17). Morocco's National Plan to Increase Tourism Competitiveness. Retrieved March 4, 2019, from https://www.moroccoworldnews.com/2016/08/194411/moroccos-national-plan-increase-tourism-competitiveness/.
39 Muslim Village.com. (2014, September 3). "Halal' Swimsuits Banned in Morocco". Retrieved March 7, 2019, from https://muslimvillage.com/2014/09/03/57431/halal-swimsuits-banned-in-morocco/.
40 Karam, S. (2012, July 2). "Maiden Gay Cruise to Muslim Land Hits Morocco Snag". *Reuters.* Retrieved February 15, 2019, from https://www.reuters.com/article/uk-morocco-gay-cruiseship/maiden-gay-cruise-to-muslim-land-hits-morocco-snag-idUSLNE86100L20120702.
41 Jing, G. (2016, December 5). "Morocco to Offer Visa-free Travel for Chinese Tourists". China Radio International Service (CRI). Retrieved March 5, 2019, from http://english.cri.cn/12394/2016/05/12/2743s927365.htm.
42 Ibid.
43 Jacobs, H. (2019, February 7). "One of Morocco's Top Tourist Destinations Has Become Overrun with Tourists and Instagrammers Trying to Get the Perfect Photo". *Business Insider.* Retrieved from https://www.businessinsider.com/marrakech-morocco-majorelle-garden-tourists-instagrammers-2019-2.
44 China.Org.com. (2019, February 15). Retrieved March 5, 2019, from http://www.china.org.cn/world/Off_the_Wire/2019-02/15/content_74469980.htm.
45 Ibid.
46 Wikipedia, "Casablanca-Tangier High Speed Rail." Retrieved March 5, 2019, from https://en.wikipedia.org/wiki/Casablanca%E2%80%93Tangier_high-speed_rail_line.
47 Blogarama. (2017, April 7). "Mohamed Sajid – Morocco's New Minister of Tourism". Retrieved March 5, 2019, from https://www.blogarama.com/arts-and-entertainment-blogs/15264-view-from-fez-blog/19956928-mohamed-sajid-moroccos-new-minister-tourism.
48 Yabiladi in English. (2018, July 13). "Rising Oil Prices to Affect Morocco's Economy, Says the Government." Retrieved March 5, 2019, from https://en.yabiladi.com/articles/details/67033/rising-prices-affect-morocco-s-economy.html.

8 King Mohammed VI's economic development strategies

Twenty years have passed since King Mohammed VI assumed Morocco's throne. As no mere constitutional monarch, but rather a Monarch with real political and economic power, the King has played an active role in the economic development choices of his country. It is the argument of this book that the King chose an economic development strategy that did not neatly fit with the national-level strategies that were being promoted prior to his assumption of the throne. King Mohammed VI did not fully embrace a neoliberal model of economic development, nor did he pursue a model of essentially state-led development.

Rather the King's choices reflect a three-pronged development strategy that included (1) a focus on sectoral development that over time diversified Morocco's production and its export destinations as well as diversifying its target population of tourists to Morocco. The King also insisted on trainings and workshops to professionalize managers and service delivery staff in every sector; (2) an effort to leapfrog the technologies in key sectors in which Morocco engaged; and (3) the adoption of Morocco's own "variety of capitalism" model in which neoliberal principles are ubiquitous, but in which state interventions guide development and/or intervene in the vagaries of the market to support some social justice concerns for Moroccan citizens, address private corporate needs, engage in public–private partnerships, and work to maintain political peace as a necessary factor for promoting development.

Sectoral development and diversification of export destinations

In the King's sectoral approaches to economic development, public–private partnerships play an important role in securing the necessary investment and professional knowledge to develop a sector. State guaranteed tax holidays, land, and the development of a world class transit and logistics system also assisted the country's ability to convince producers to locate in Morocco. So, too, did the promise of stable domestically produced energy. All of these state activities in addition to Morocco's geographical position and low-wage employment were critical to accelerating Morocco's economic development.

At the insistence of the King and his ministers, copious trainings and workshops were undertaken during the first ten years of King Mohammed VI's reign to professionalize those working in targeted sectors. This approach, as noted in Chapter 2, was especially successfully in the finance sector where a modern, expert group of officials and staff had to interface with foreign investors. But the professionalization of management, service, and production line employees in all of Morocco's targeted development sectors also was important to the country's economic expansion as well. These trainings tracked well with the World Bank "good governance" policies that became popular in the 1990s when international development consultants came to recognize that markets do not function properly if government officials cannot perform their administrative responsibilities.

Further, King Mohammed VI chose to develop sectors mainly where Morocco already had some production capabilities, where the country's geographical position gave it a comparative advantage, or where its reputation and heritage sites (in the tourism sector) could attract new customers.

As noted in Chapter 4, new productive endeavors introduced by foreign investors such as Renault were pursued by the King and the country's representatives. Once secured, Renault was regarded as an original equipment manufacturer (OEM) and it then spurred other overseas manufacturers to locate branches in Morocco and small- and medium-sized Moroccan enterprises to produce for Renault. Morocco aspires to work to replicate this model with other major producers.

With Morocco's varied climate and terrain, glorious history and cultural heritage, Morocco's tourism sector was targeted for expansion as well. Already a source of much-needed foreign exchange, hotels were upgraded, roads and transport vehicles were improved, and younger, astute technocrats were named to guide the tourism ministry. After some time, the ministry itself was redesigned to integrate many of the supporting components of tourism such as air transit and handicrafts.

Morocco's portfolio of exports during the past 20 years has included an expansion in the numbers of cars, agriculture products, and textiles targeted for the European market. But the King also energetically has sought, and continues to seek, new markets for Morocco's goods that include exports regionally in sub-Saharan Africa, the Middle East, and North Africa, as well as exports to economic powers like the United States, China, and Russia.

In fact, building on its cutting-edge logistics and geographical position, Morocco has sought to position itself as a financial and transit hub between Africa and economic powers on other continents. As of March 2019, Morocco had concluded or updated about 60 free trade agreements with other countries. King Mohammed VI was largely responsible for this feat. As Morocco's Minister of Investment and Industry, Moulay Hafid Elalamy, noted, "This has allowed us to position ourselves as an indispensable African platform for investments, production, and exportation opportunities."[1]

Thus, Morocco has looked to major producers in Africa as well as to other new and important economies for new productive exchanges. For example, in 2015, Morocco and India signed new trade agreements. India hopes to import Morocco's phosphates for use in fertilizer in support of the Indian agricultural sector that works to provide sufficient food for an enormous population. In exchange, Indian exports to Morocco include chemicals, automobiles, medicines, and cotton yarn. Following the 2015 agreement, new market niches for Morocco to gain trade from India now include film-making and tourist travel. And both India and Morocco see Morocco's contacts and knowledge in Africa as helpful for facilitating Indian investment in the continent. Expanding contacts with rising powers, like India, has clearly been part of King Mohamed VI's development strategy.

By 2013, trade between China and Morocco had reached $2.3 billion. Morocco's exports to China consisted mainly of minerals, fertilizers, and metals – all produced by large Moroccan industries.[2] And we know that in 2016, when China and Morocco signed a free trade agreement, some feared that cheaply produced Chinese goods would flood Morocco and prevent Moroccan entrepreneurs from establishing and sustaining new businesses. Others said that Chinese goods in the Moroccan market would force Moroccans to learn to compete in global markets and would allow Moroccan consumers to purchase more goods because many Chinese goods cost less than comparable Moroccan goods.[3]

In 2017, the latest figures that are available, note the direction of Morocco's exports to the following countries: 22% of Morocco's exports went to France and 22% of them went to Spain.

Other export destinations included Germany 4.6(%), Italy 4.5(%), the United States 4.4(%), Turkey 3.6(%), the United Kingdom 3.2(%), and Brazil 3.0(%).

Still another tier of exports went to India 2.9(%), China 2.5(%), Russia 2.1(%), the Netherlands 1.5(%), Poland 1.5(%), Belgium–Luxembourg 1.4(%), Japan 1.2(%), Switzerland 1.1(%), and Algeria 1.0(%).

And the final notable group of exports went to Pakistan 0.95(%), Austria 0.79(%), South Korea 0.73(%), Nigeria 0.56(%), Indonesia 0.50(%), Singapore 0.48(%), Tunisia 0.48(%), Ghana 0.46(%), Egypt 0.44(%), Hong Kong 0.44(%), Senegal 0.41(%), Norway 0.34(%), Mali 0.30(%), South Africa 0.29(%), and Cameroon 0.28(%), with Cameroon representing $70 million of export value.[4]

Morocco has deliberately sought to enter free trade pacts with countries beyond those of Europe or the United States. In the second decade of the King's reign, Brazil, Russia, India, China, and South Africa – the BRICS – were targeted. And so, Brazil, Russia, India, China, and South Africa all concluded free trade agreements with Morocco, allowing the Kingdom to engage with emerging economic powers and to diversify somewhat from its dependence on Western Europe.

But trade deals take time to negotiate and more time to implement. For example, the Agadir Agreement among Morocco, Egypt, Jordan, and Tunisia was announced in May 2001. After sustained negotiations, it was signed in 2004. The agreement came into force in March 2007.

It had been hoped that the Agadir Agreement would bring together the four countries so they could further the integration of the European Union (EU)-Mediterranean process. But the events of the Arab spring in both Egypt and Tunisia prevented necessary addendums and memorandums from being worked out.

Additionally, sometimes it is difficult to negotiate trade agreements that will run simultaneously. For example, the Agadir Agreement used definitions of country and rules of origin that were compatible with the EU.[5] But Morocco had signed a free trade agreement with the United States in 2004 and it went into force in 2006. The US-Moroccan agreement utilized an alternative definition of country and rules of origin for Morocco's trade.[6] New negotiations and procedures had to be negotiated among the Agadir group.

It would do no good to expand sectoral production and have no market in which to sell the goods produced. Thus, Morocco's sectoral development and its trade diversification have been part of an integrated strategy. However, to support its expanding production of goods, Morocco's economic development strategies also have paid close attention to the integration of new practices and technologies for producing goods and services.

The King's decision to leapfrog to cutting-edge technologies in the key sectors in which Morocco produces

With regard to adopting technologies, King Mohammed VI and his advisors did not attempt to reinvent the wheel. Rather, as Chapter 5 so vividly describes with respect to sustainable energy, they studied and imported the latest technologies, including technologies just on the cusp of production. These technologies were adopted for Morocco's development in ways that positioned Morocco well for the future. "We are at the avante-garde of solar" stated Maha el-Kadiri, a Moroccan Agency for Sustainable Energy (MASEN) spokeswoman for Morocco's "largest concentrated solar power (CSP) plant in the world."[7]

And while Morocco's adoption of leapfrog technology practices often positioned it well for the future, sometimes, as with many new technological approaches, early adoption is costly. This was especially true in the adoption of Morocco's solar power production in the Saharan desert. The cost for Morocco's solar power plans is $9 billion and some critics worry that the money will never be recouped. Others believe it will be recouped through exporting energy to Europe and to neighboring states.

Additionally, there was some debate on using the water that the steam pipes heated by the solar panels use. Some in the agricultural sector were very concerned about securing their share of access to water. They feared that huge quantities of water would be diverted from agricultural production. But it turns out that the Noor solar complex and other solar panel energy sites in Morocco have spurred entrepreneurs to find new solutions that can help farmers. As discussed below, Ismail Bouhamidi, a young

Moroccan, has created his own firm, "Fellah PRO" that harnesses solar energy to irrigate agricultural fields through floating solar water pumps.[8] And as Project Drawdown has noted,

> Hot water for showers, laundry, and washing dishes consumes a quarter of residential energy use worldwide; in commercial buildings, that number is roughly 12 percent. Solar water heating – exposing water to the sun to warm it – can reduce that fuel consumption by 50 to 70 percent.[9]

Many hope that Morocco, after learning the production of solar energy for Noor, will successfully adopt such technologies to provide hot running water for citizens across Morocco.

And by almost every measure, Morocco's solar accomplishment is stunning. Noor I, the first of Morocco's four plants outside the city of Ouarzazate, was certified operative in February 2016.[10] Until Noor ("light" in Arabic) was built, Ouarzazate was known as a film venue where projects like "Game of Thrones," "Gladiator," and "Lawrence of Arabia" were filmed.

But Noor I now functions well and at least seven more plants are scheduled and under construction.

And as the British newspaper the Guardian noted:

> in 1986 the German particle physicist Gerhard Knies calculated that the world's deserts receive enough energy in a few hours to provide for humanity's power needs for a whole year. The challenge though, has been capturing that energy and transporting it to the population centres where it is required.[11]

Thus, extraordinary excitement was generated around King Mohammed VI's decision to leapfrog technologies and endorse solar and other forms of non-carbon producing energy. As analyzed in Chapter 5, MASEN's plan for renewable energy entails building four gigantic solar sites near Ouarzazate, and then one each at Boujdourm, Sebkha Tah, Ain Beni Mathar, and Foum El Oued. These are envisioned to be complete by 2020, though many acknowledge a few may come on line a bit late. But Noor I is a major success. And unlike the traditional use of photovoltaic cells in Europe and elsewhere, Morocco is using parabolic mirrors to generate heat for conventional steam turbines.

The technology for this proposal resulted from a joint venture of "the Desertec Industrial Initiative (DII), a coalition of companies including E.ON, Siemens, Munich Re and Deutsche Bank" that announced its plans with Morocco in 2011.[12] The goal was not only to provide Morocco with an energy alternative to its dependence on oil but also to export energy to Europe and provide the continent with 15% of Europe's electricity supply by 2050.[13]

Further, as noted in Chapter 2 that analyzes Morocco's financial development, MASEN was given permission, in conjunction with the Morocco government and in consultation with its bank, to issue Green Bonds that were guaranteed by the Moroccan government. Green bonds are innovative financial instruments that attract investors in projects that promote sustainable energy projects whether the projects target entire countries or whether those projects target local communities.

The excitement surrounding Morocco's use of solar power also promoted a climate of opportunity that has created (spin offs of) other new technologies. Ismail Bouhamidi, a young Moroccan who earned a Diploma in Agricultural Engineering, created his own firm, "Fellah PRO" that harnesses solar energy to irrigate agricultural fields through floating solar water pumps. As of 2019, Bouhamidi already has employed staff to help with his company and his Casablanca-based Project Manager noted that the "solar water pump is affordable, highly efficient and is customized according to the needs of the farmer."[14] Additionally, taking advantage of Morocco's new telecommunications technology, an IPhone app allows Bouhamidi to run the business.[15]

Excited, young, skilled entrepreneurs who find ways to help development are critical for Morocco. By leapfrogging technology and providing new financial services, King Mohammed VI has created a national climate that welcomes innovation and may well inspire dozens of entrepreneurs like Bouhamidi to bring their skills home.

Another of Morocco's leapfrog innovations can be found in the tourist sector, as discussed in Chapter 7, where the country's eco-tourism projects incorporate the best new practices of eco-tourism in the world. Likewise, Morocco's new ports and container technology, discussed in Chapter 4, are both cutting edge and large in scale. Morocco's goal is to transform its "Tanger Med" container port into the biggest container port in Africa.[16] And leaders of the country's transport and logistics sector released a new Industrial Acceleration Plan (PAI) for the 2014–2020 period setting the goal of stimulating growth and focusing on exports from the agricultural, aeronautics, automobile, textiles, and pharmaceutical sectors. The plan hopes to stimulate the export of more Moroccan-made products as well as to serve as a transit hub for goods passing from one continent to another.

Morocco's leadership in technological innovation for a country of its size has been noted internationally. The 2017 Global Innovation Index (GII) demonstrated that "Morocco leads North Africa and is among the top ten countries in its income bracket" for technological innovation.[17] The GII study is conducted and coauthored by Cornell University, INSEAD and the World Intellectual Property Organization.

The Moroccan American Center for Policy (MACP) that tracks Morocco's initiatives and accomplishments, noted that the 2017 Bloomberg Innovation Index named Morocco as one of the 50 most innovative economies in the world.[18] MACP also noted the "KPMG International and Oxford

Economics" 2015 Change Readiness Index (CRI) ranked Morocco as the most "change-ready" country in the Maghreb, with particularly positive results in the category of "enterprise capability."[19] Morocco has garnered other accolades as well for leapfrogging and utilizing innovative technologies across its development sectors.

Morocco's innovation technologies offer the promise of accomplishing goals while also achieving independence from other countries or markets. But innovation technologies, because they are new, must be incorporated at a slower rate than technologies that are known and can be applied rapidly following earlier installation procedures. Therefore, the completion of a product and the benefits and ripple effects of new technologies often come slowly.

The adoption of Morocco's own variety of capitalism

As for choosing its own variety of capitalism approach, Morocco mostly supported market conditions for its producers and workers but intervened to guide development through making capital accessible in targeted areas for new productive enterprises and also by offering a social safety net through subsidies that cost the state revenues. This was an approach the state would not have undertaken if it took the advice of many international advisers to rid the state of all debt, even at great cost to its people. The King clearly recognizes that political stability is needed in order for the state to attract foreign investment to develop. And Morocco's variety of capitalism also rests largely on King Mohammed VI's insistence on professional trainings for those working in Morocco's targeted development sectors.

The "varieties of capitalism" debates in Europe grew out of the work of those who studied political economies in Europe and began to challenge the image of an evolving single model of a Western inspired capitalist political economy in the post-Cold World period. Instead, "varieties of capitalism" researchers argued that even among Western European states, there are many variations in the forms of capitalism across Europe. In many European countries, it became clear that a variety of entrepreneurs and corporations were important actors in those countries. As Bob Hancké explained it, in many studies of European development, the business firm remained the central unit of analysis.[20] From the firm's perspective, scholars and practitioners analyzed the firm's relations with labor, the state, those in the market who purchased the firm's goods and services, the banks and other sources of capital from whom the firms borrowed, the suppliers of goods (mainly tools and technology) to firms, and the markets for purchasing those goods in which firms needed to participate in order to produce their own products.[21]

Western "varieties of capitalism" researchers investigated the markets and state institutions that structured relations and markets for firms in order to determine which forms among the existing "varieties of capitalism" led to the best outcomes for a firm's success in the modern globalizing economy. Other researchers and practitioners analyzed innovations that enabled a firm to continue to compete globally. But ultimately, researchers sought to answer the question, as David Coates has posed it, "why some...capitalist economies have performed better than others."[22]

Colin Crouch alternatively has observed that while the "varieties of capitalism" debates may have evolved with an emphasis on the firm, "theories of capitalist diversity...usually originated in studies of the labour market and social policy" as well as studies of "institutionalism."[23] Further, Crouch noted that the World Bank and OECD argued that only those countries with business, state, and labor institutions that remained "close to the market" provided the dynamism needed for a country's economic development.[24] So, scholars concluded that countries that encouraged state intervention still need a healthy free market if a country's economic planners were successfully to promote development.

Other researchers, however, redirected the unit of analysis away from the focus on the firm. A number of "varieties of capitalism" researchers focused on the lives of workers and trade unions within various states while others began asking how the varieties of capitalism in a globalizing world were now affecting middle management individuals in large firms and what impact that had on the human resources practices in those firms.[25]

When Mohammed VI assumed the throne in Morocco, his approach to economic development can be seen as what development scholars would call Morocco's version of a variety of capitalism. For Morocco, it is clear that King Mohammed VI did not adopt either a completely neoliberal market strategy for Moroccan development or complete state intervention and planning. The King and his advisers were interested in targeting and developing Morocco by sectors.

In general, Morocco's strategy allowed corporations to stay close to the market in order to spur development as noted above by those who studied the conditions for development. Thus, Morocco's own "variety of capitalism" model allowed neoliberal principles to obtain where markets could flourish. But Moroccan officials reserved the right for state interventions to guide development and intervene in markets in order to provide some social safety nets for Moroccan citizens, to assist productive enterprises in targeted sectors, and also to address some social justice concerns for Moroccans.

Moreover, state leaders insisted on trainings and workshops to professionalize managers and service delivery staff in every sector. And Moroccan state leaders monitored their target sectors to see that the workshops took place. Further, state development leaders insisted that the upgrading of professional skills occur in both private and public enterprises. The King and his ministers wanted to modernize the country's development sectors and also have those sectors staffed by well-trained workers. As an added benefit, they also received credit and support from development specialists at the World Bank and other international organization for promoting "good governance" through their efforts to upgrade the skills of Moroccans working in their targeted development sectors.

Morocco's variety of capitalism also aimed for targeted sectors to adopt leapfrog technologies so that Moroccans could compete in a globalized market. As discussed above, King Mohammed VI aimed to make Morocco a leader, not simply to advance its economic development technologies. Moroccan Green Bonds were created, solar power achieved, eco-sustainable tourist sites developed, etc. Additionally, Morocco's transportation and container shipping sector adopted state-of-the-art technologies.

Unlike the European models of varieties of capitalism, Morocco's variety of capitalism focuses less on private companies and their labor relations or their relations with the state than it does on sectoral development. The rights of corporations and/or workers are not a priority in those sectors that have been targeted for Moroccan development. In fact, when laying the foundation for development in Morocco, a key goal for the King and his advisers appears to be that a citizen should obtain a job; rarely over the past 20 years, has one heard the King or his Ministers address working conditions or wages, except following outbursts when thousands of Moroccans take to the streets.

However, there exist basic laws that offer some protection to Moroccan workers. According to article 143 of the Moroccan Labor Code, children must be 15 years old before they can be employed.[26] They must be 18 years old before they may be hired for dangerous work that risks their health or life.[27]

Morocco has a schedule regarding when wages must be paid (weekly, monthly, etc.) for each kind of enterprise. Additionally, in July 2015, the Moroccan government established a national minimum wage for work: "13,46 Moroccan Dirhams per hour in commercial and industrial sector and 69,73 Moroccan Dirhams per day in the agriculture sector."[28] In March 2019, these wages were equal to $1.40 and $7.27, respectively. One has to wonder, what were Moroccan workers earning previously? And if Morocco's workers are making such low salaries now, after initiating the new 2015 wage law, how can a demand structure to purchase Moroccan produced goods be instituted in the country where many workers have little discretionary income?

Granted, these figures represent the very low end of Moroccan workers' pay scales. But 25% of the Moroccan population is earning less than 10,250 Moroccan dirhams a month – or about $1,025 a month (25% are earning more than 30,000 Moroccan dirhams a month or $3,000).[29] Yet, Moroccan citizens must make many of their purchases in a global economy, paying global prices.

And as the Employment Law Alliance CWA Morocco notes,

> Overtime is paid at an increase on the hourly rate of 25% for hours worked between 6:00 a.m. to 7:00 p.m. in the non-agricultural sector and 5:00 a.m. to 8:00 p.m. in the agricultural sector. The rate is increased to 50% if the overtime hours were carried out between 9:00 p.m. and 6:00 a.m. in the non-agricultural sector and 8:00 p.m. to 5:00 a.m. in the agricultural sector.[30]

Clearly, wages and workers have not been the focus of Morocco's economic development efforts and appear to lack priority in Morocco's version of a variety of capitalism model of development.

Morocco's model of development is a variety of *capitalism* model because the free market and other neoliberal policies play major roles. However, the Moroccan development model is a *variety* of capitalism because, as noted above, King Mohamed VI has been willing to violate neoliberal principles and offer subsidies when Morocco's workers and unemployed come into the streets and demand food and shelter.

The state also provides for capitalist enterprises that will locate and produce in Morocco. Tax holidays, infrastructure, and labor quiescence are attractive incentives for recruited producers. And within the parameters of Morocco's variety of capitalism, the state also partners with producers in its targeted sectors so that the costs of an investment, and the risks of a new investment, are shared.

But as we noted in Chapter 6, it is a commonly held belief that Morocco has one economy for the well-connected who can find jobs, and a second economy for those with no access to decision-makers, and thus no access to jobs. And Moroccan citizens are not alone in their beliefs. In 2019, even in the Western capitalist countries, debates about the nature of capitalism are taking place. For example, one journal, *Forbes*, long a bastion of US capitalism and corporate reference, published a special issue in 2019 that ran an article on "reimagining capitalism." In it, Paul Tudor Jones, a famous US hedge fund investor, argued that

> Unless we find a market-based solution to the expanding growth in inequality, we will end up with populist legislation that creates a hammer to go after every nail.[31]

In *Forbes'* special edition, Jones was not alone in his concerns that those who have achieved great wealth, and those in public office, need to focus on more than just profit margins for individual firms. And just as Western capitalists need to pause and consider such issues, Moroccan corporate and government leaders also would be wise to find ways to address the inequalities that persist in Morocco.

Morocco's economy after two decades of rule (1999–2019) by King Mohammed VI

King Mohammed VI has accelerated the development of several of Morocco's sectors. Of special note are finance, telecommunications, tourism, sustainable energy, and transit and trade. Additionally, over the past 20 years, the King has worked energetically to enter into economic partnerships with countries across Africa and with countries with leading economies as well as with those countries who have emerging economies.

But, unfortunately, as the data show, Morocco has not become as productive, or created as many jobs, as the King and his advisers had hoped. Thus, it appears that for many Moroccans, it is their children or grandchildren, who will benefit from Morocco's trajectory in development. Even for the next generation, however, there exist no guarantees.

Additionally, Morocco's development has been geographically uneven. Morocco's leaders need to focus their attention on creating urban–rural production and sales linkages that can assist development in Morocco's rural regions. It is unlikely that foreigner investors will prefer to locate in rural areas. Developing Morocco's rural areas will need strategic intervention by state leaders.

Morocco's economy is still dependent on good rains for its agriculture. Additionally, Morocco's economy would do better if all of its resources were directed toward productive enterprises and not diverted into the pockets of those who already have secured fortunes. Moreover, the informal taxes that many Moroccans must pay in order to obtain their licenses and other official documents, slows development.

Morocco is also dependent for its new trade agreements on the relationships that the King has worked to establish with leaders of other countries. But those relationships could shift.

For example, King Mohammed VI has found common ground with certain leaders across Africa and the Middle East who are hoping that Morocco can function as a facilitator for foreign investors coming into their countries even as the two countries expand their own trade with one another. Morocco has been investing or bringing investment to African countries such as Nigeria, Senegal, Egypt, Ethiopia, and Cameroon to develop phosphate plants, for which Morocco possesses expertise, or in Nigeria's case to assist with the development of an oil pipeline that will run through Moroccan territory. Morocco's own companies, many owned by those close to the King, have invested in other country's markets in the telecommunications and other sectors. In South Sudan, agriculture, mining, and tourism are the main development areas in which South Sudan is expecting assistance from Morocco.

Such economic statecraft has not only assisted in Morocco's economic development but also gained the country allies in the region. Morocco earned its way back into the African Union in 2017, as noted in Chapter 2. Through his economic statecraft, King Mohammed VI persuaded many African state leaders to overlook his country's position regarding the Western Sahara. Like Morocco's King, many African state leaders are looking for any avenues they can pursue to achieve economic development for their populations. But state leaders who do not prioritize opposing Morocco's position on the Western Sahara could be replaced by those who do. So, relationships must be nurtured over time.

Under King Mohammed VI's plans for economic development, Morocco, traditionally, has leaned to the West, but diversified to other powers and engaged in trade and aid with other regions. United States Lt. Col. Winston Tierney, the lead planner for joint US and Moroccan military exercises in 2018, was quoted in 2019 when those exercises (African Lion 2019) reoccurred. From the US perspective, he noted, "This robust, reliable relationship is the cornerstone to shaping the security environment in the region."[32] Under King Mohammed VI, Morocco has been a staunch ally of the West in combatting terrorism.

Yet, Morocco also is a country along China's Belt and Road Initiative (BRI). To project trade and power, China has purchased the operational rights to many ports around the world and these include a presence in Morocco. Further, Russia has four diplomatic sites in Morocco. Morocco looks to Russia for tourists and business investment. In March 2016, King Mohammed VI traveled to Russia to meet with Vladamir Putin. Their talks resulted in plans for more air travel and tourism between the two countries, and agreements on fishing that increased access by Russian fishermen to Morocco's fisheries by 8% or 10,500 tons.[33]

King Mohammed VI has carefully woven a network of allies and those with whom he can do business. But should anything happen to King Mohammed VI, it is unclear what would happen to Morocco's development trajectory.

In September 17, 2017, King Mohammed VI was hospitalized for eye surgery and then for heart surgery in February 2018. The King has two children: his son Prince Moulay Hassan who was born in May 2003, and a younger daughter, Princess Lalla Khadija. Prince Moulay Hasan is the heir apparent but obviously, at his age, he is not up to the work that his father does. Prince Moulay Rachid, the younger brother of King Mohammed VI, is second in line for throne. He was born in 1970.

Should anything happen to Morocco's King Mohammed VI, would the country, under the leadership of a less powerful and younger King, or led by the younger brother of the present King, continue to aggressively lay the foundation, sector by sector, for Morocco's development? Could another Moroccan King manage to balance and maintain the country's new trading partners? Few other leaders have so single mindedly, and with such energy, pursued economic development for their country as has King Mohammed VI of Morocco.

Historically, 20 years is a short period of time. But for a Moroccan citizen who was 30 years old when King Mohammed VI assumed the throne in 1999, 20 years may well be the better part of that person's lifespan. And in 2019, there has been little change over the past 20 years for the vast majority of Moroccans, or for their sons and daughters.

King Mohammed VI's development accomplishments over the past 20 years, however, have brought changes to Morocco and have made an important difference in the country's prospects for the future. The King's economic development accomplishments have prodded Morocco toward a path of development that contains good prospects for future success.

Clearly more needs to be done, and importantly, Morocco's leaders need to pay attention to the distribution of the benefits of development success as it occurs. Additionally, those who value Morocco, and hope for its success, must work to support King Mohammed VI's development strategies so that all Moroccans may begin to reap the dividends of the foundational work for economic development that has been laid during the last two decades.

Notes

1 Koundouno, T. F. (2019, March 18). "Morocco Positions Itself in Pioneering Role in Indian-African Relations". *Morocco World News*. Retrieved from https://www.moroccoworldnews.com/2019/03/268349/morocco-pioneering-role-indian-african-relations/.
2 Mayer, S. (2016, June 24). "Morocco Enters Free Trade Pact with China". *Africa-ME*. Retrieved from http://africa-me.com/morocco-enters-free-trade-pact-china/.
3 Ibid.
4 Observatory of Economic Complexity. Retrieved from https://atlas.media.mit.edu/en/profile/country/mar/ is the source of data for all the 2017 exports listed in this section.
5 Bilaterals.org the "Agadir Agreement". Retrieved from https://www.bilaterals.org/?-agadir-agreement- (bilaterals.org was initiated in September 2004 by the Asia-Pacific Research Network, GATT Watchdog, Global Justice Ecology Project, GRAIN, IBON Foundation and XminusY).
6 Ibid.
7 Neslen, A. (2015, October 26). "Morocco Poised to Become a Solar Superpower with Launch of Desert Mega-Project". *The Guardian*. Retrieved March 9, 2019, from https://www.theguardian.com/environment/2015/oct/26/morocco-poised-to-become-a-solar-superpower-with-launch-of-desert-mega-project?utm_source=The+Overspill&utm_campaign=41853dcb34-daily-email&utm_medium=email&utm_term=0_7256cb1804-41853dcb34-156236589.
8 Boughanmi, O. (2017, July 10). "Fellah PRO Renewable Energy and Energy Efficiency" FellahPRO blog. Retrieved March 10, 2019, from https://www.theswitchers.eu/en/switchers/morocco-is-reviving-the-agricultural-system-floating-solar-panels/.
9 Project Drawdown. (n.d.). "Electricity Generation Solar Water". Retrieved from https://www.drawdown.org/solutions/electricity-generation/solar-water.
10 Fritzenkotter, J. (2016, February 4). "NoorI"SoMed!. Retrieved March 10, 2018, from http://so-med.org/content/Noor-i.
11 Op cit. Neslen, A. "Morocco Poised to Become a Solar Superpower with Launch of Desert Mega-Project".
12 Hickman L., & Gersmann, H. (2011, November 2). "Morocco to Host First Solar Farm in €400bn Renewables Network". *Guardian*. Retrieved March 10, 2019, from https://www.theguardian.com/environment/2011/nov/02/morocco-solar-farm-renewables.
13 Ibid.
14 Ibid. Boughanmi, O. "Fellah PRO Renewable Energy and Energy Efficiency".
15 Ibid.
16 "Tanger Med to Transform into Biggest Container Port in Africa". (2016, December 13) *African Business*. Cited in *Morocco World News*. Retrieved March 10, 2019, from https://www.moroccoworldnews.com/2016/12/203649/tanger-med-to-transform-into-biggest-container-port-in-africa-magazine/.

17 "Morocco Leads North Africa in Latest Global Innovation Index". (June 19, 2017) *Businesswire*. Retrieved March 10, 2019, from https://www.businesswire. com/news/home/20170619006113/en/Morocco-Leads-North-Africa-Latest-Global-Innovation.

18 Ibid.

19 Ibid.

20 Hanckè, B. ed. (2009). *Debating Varieties of Capitalism* (Oxford: Oxford University Press).

21 Ibid.

22 Coates, D. (2005). *Varieties of Capitalism, Varieties of Approaches* (Basingstoke and New York: Palgrave Macmillan).

23 Crouch, C. (2012). "National Varieties of Labour in Market Exposure" in Glenn Morgan and Richard Whitley, eds. *Capitalisms and Capitalism in the Twenty-First Century* (Oxford: Oxford University Press), p. 90.

24 Ibid.

25 See for example, Lewin, D. ed. (2006). *Contemporary Issues in Employment Relations* (Champaign, IL: Labor and Employment Relations Association) especially the chapters Cutcher-Gershenfeld, J., Sleigh, S. R., & Pil, F. K. "Collective Bargaining: Keeping Score on a Great American Institution" and Levine, D. I., & Lewin, D. "The New 'Managerial Misclassification' Challenge to Old Wage and Hour Law; or, What Is Managerial Work?" Also see Katz, H. C., & Darbishire, O. (2000). *Converging Divergences Worldwide Changes in Employment Systems* (Ithaca, NY: International Labor Relations Press/Cornell University Press).

26 Employment Law Alliance CWA Morocco, "Morocco Labor and Employment Law". *Global Employers Handbook*. Retrieved from https://www.ela.law/ globalemployerhandbook/morocco.

27 Ibid.

28 Ibid.

29 Salary Explorer in Morocco. Retrieved from http://www.salaryexplorer.com/ salary-survey.php?loc=146&loctype=1; conversion of currency was done at Bing Currency Converter. https://www.bing.com/search?q=convert%20moroccan% 20currency%20to%20dollars&pc=cosp&ptag=G6C999N1234D020118A98 C4AF66BD&form=CONBDF&conlogo=CT3210127.

30 Op cit. Employment Law Alliance CWA Morocco, "Morocco Labor and Employment Law". *Global Employers Handbook*.

31 Lane, R. (2019, March 4). "The World's Billionaires Reimagining Capitalism". *Forbes*.

32 Kasraoui, S. (2019, March 19). "Morocco-US Joint Military Exercise Kicks Off in Southern Morocco". *Morocco World News*. Retrieved from https:// www.moroccoworldnews.com/2019/03/268259/morocco-us-joint-military-exercise-southern-morocco/.

33 Oudrhiri, Z. (2019, February 22). "Morocco and Russia Expand Deal on Fishing off Sahara Coast". *Morocco World News*. Retrieved from https://www. moroccoworldnews.com/2019/02/266462/morocco-russia-deal-fishing-sahara-coast/.

Index

For Product Safety Concerns and Information please contact our EU
representative GPSR@taylorandfrancis.com
Taylor & Francis Verlag GmbH, Kaufingerstraße 24, 80331 München, Germany